Just Who Do You Say You Are?

A Word Study of Who GOD Says You Are

Just Who Do You Say You Are?

A Word Study of Who GOD Says You Are

Noreen Sergent

CHP

Just Who Do You Say You Are? by Noreen Sergent
Published by Creation House Press (CHP)
A Charisma Media Company
600 Rinehart Road
Lake Mary, Florida 32746
www.charismamedia.com

Design Director: Bill Johnson
Cover design by Terry Clifton

Library of Congress Cataloging-in-Publication Data:
2013930876
International Standard Book Number: 978-1-62136-350-7
E-book International Standard Book Number:
978-1-62136-351-4

14 15 16 17 18 — 98765432
Printed in the United States of America

TABLE OF CONTENTS

INTRODUCTION

I BEGAN TO STUDY who I am in Christ after hearing a preacher by the name of Isaac Pitre on Trinity Broadcasting Network. He said something that I'd never heard before, or if I had it had not resonated with me as it did that night. He spoke of how after we accept Jesus as our Lord, as we grow in Him we should be looking just like Him. Jesus came to this earth to show us how we should be living. It is in Him, through Him, by Him—all in Christ. Unfortunately most of us have the belief that our old nature will not change until we see Jesus face-to-face. However I became so provoked by what Pitre taught that I began to study the Word (Bible) and find out what God had to say about us being in Christ. As I began to study what God has to say about me and who I am in Him, my thoughts about myself had to change. My thoughts began to line up with the Word!

I did this study mostly from the New Testament, for that is where we begin in this new creation or new covenant. Jesus is the New Covenant and I believe as you read and discover who you are in Him your life will change and be so full of God that you will never want to go back to the old you. The Triune God—God the Father, God the Son, and God the Holy Spirit—truly dwell in us as soon as we accept Jesus as our Savior. Much of how you grow in the Lord depends on how much you learn by reading His Word as well as talking with Him. He is speaking to each and every one of us every day; we just have to listen.

I began this study from Colossians 1:26–27, in which Paul writes that the mystery so long hidden is Christ within us—Jesus in you and me! This really became alive to me.

> Thy mystery of which was hidden for ages, and generations [from angels and men], but is now revealed to His holy people (the saints), To whom God was pleased to make known how great for the Gentiles are the riches of the glory of this mystery, which is Christ within and among you, the Hope of [realizing the] glory.
>
> —COLOSSIANS 1:26–27

Only I have heard it taught that no one will know the Hope of Glory until we see Him face-to-face. But I heard Benny Hinn teach that Christ in you is the hidden mystery and He is the Hope of Glory! Therefore Christ in us is a right-now Person and we can know Him now, not just when we get to heaven.

Then I went to John 17:14–24:

> I have given and delivered to them your word (message) and the world has hated them, because they are not of the world [do not belong to the world], just as I am not of the world. I do not ask that You will take them out of the world, but that You will keep and protect them from the evil one. They are not of the world (worldly, belonging to the world), [just] as I am not of the world. Sanctify them [purify, consecrate, separate them for Yourself, make them holy] by Truth; Your Word is Truth. Just as You sent Me into the world, I also have sent them into the world. And so for their sake and on their behalf I sanctify (dedicate, consecrate) Myself, that they also may be sanctified (dedicated, consecrated, made holy) in the Truth. Neither for these alone do I pray [it is not for their sake only that I make this request], but also for all those who will ever come to believe in (trust in, cling to, rely on) Me through their word and teaching, That they all may be one, [just] as You, Father, are

> in Me and I in You, that they also may be one in Us, so that the world may believe and be convinced that You have sent me. I have given to them the glory and honor which You have given Me, that they may be one [even] as We are one: I in them and You in Me, in order that they may become one and perfectly united, that the world may know and [definitely] recognize that You sent Me and that You have loved them [even] as You have loved Me. Father, I desire that they also whom You have entrusted to Me [as Your gift to Me] may be with Me where I am, so that they may see My glory, which You have given Me [Your love gift to Me]; for You loved me before the foundation of the world.

As you begin to read and study the Word, as I have done, you will see that everything Jesus prayed for in this prayer we become in Him. God, Jesus, and the Holy Spirit dwell in us; we are dedicated, consecrated, and made holy, and we rule with Him from the heavenly realm. Through Him we are given honor and glory—all the same as what God gave Jesus! So let us begin this journey of the Word and truly find out who we are in Christ.

Chapter 1

CHRIST LIVES WITHIN YOU

FIRST LET'S LOOK at what Christ means. According to Strong's Concordance, Christ means "The Anointed One, Anointing or the anointing in us through the idea of contact; to smear or rub with oil, i.e., (by impl.) to consecrate to an office or religious service; anoint."

Now let's look at the Word and what it says about Christ in us, by Christ, through Christ, by Him, through Him, in Him, and so forth.

> And Peter said to him Aeneas, Jesus Christ (the Messiah) [now] makes you whole. Get up and make your bed! And immediately [Aeneas] stood up.
>
> —ACTS 9:34

We have to realize that Jesus didn't come to make just Aeneas whole; He came to make everyone whole!

> And Peter opened his mouth and said: Most certainly and thoroughly I now perceive and understand that God shows no partiality and is no respecter of persons, but in every nation he who venerates and has a reverential fear for God, treating Him with worshipful obedience and living uprightly, is acceptable to Him and sure of being received and welcomed [by Him].
>
> —ACTS 10:34–35

Now that is interesting. All are accepted, received, and welcomed by Him if we have a reverential fear for God, worship Him, be obedient, and live uprightly. He is Lord of all.

> For in Him we live and move and have our being; as even some of your [own] poets have said, For we are also His offspring.
>
> —Acts 17:28

> And this includes you, called of Jesus Christ and invited [as you are] to belong to Him.
>
> —Romans 1:6

We are called by Him and invited to belong to Him!

> But now the righteousness of God has been revealed independently and altogether apart from the Law, although actually it is attested by the Law and the Prophets. Namely, the righteousness of God which comes by believing with personal trust and confident reliance on Jesus Christ (the Messiah). [And it is meant] for all who believe. For there is no distinction.
>
> —Romans 3:21–22

When we accept Jesus as our Savior we become the righteousness of God.

> [All] are justified and made upright and in right standing with God, freely and gratuitously by His grace (His unmerited favor and mercy), through the redemption which is [provided] in Christ Jesus. Whom God put forward [before the eyes of all] as a mercy seat and propitiation by His blood [the cleansing and life-giving sacrifice of atonement and reconciliation, to be received] through faith. This was to show God's righteousness, because in His divine

> forbearance He had passed over and ignored former sins without punishment.
>
> —Romans 3:24–25

We are justified, made upright, in right standing with God by His free grace, redeemed by Jesus, cleansed by the blood, reconciled, and to be received by God through faith! Wow!

> For if while we were enemies we were reconciled to God through the death of His Son, it is much more [certain], now that we are reconciled, that we shall be saved (daily delivered from sin's dominion) through His [resurrection] life.
>
> —Romans 5:10–11

Wow! We are reconciled and delivered daily from sin's dominion through His resurrection. Have you ever heard that statement before? Daily delivered from sin's dominion? God says we can do this—live daily without sinning. That is why He sent His Son.

> For if because of one man's trespass (lapse, offense) death reigned through that one, much more surely will those who receive [God's] overflowing grace (unmerited favor) and the free gift of righteousness [putting them into right standing with Himself] reign as kings in life through the one Man Jesus Christ (the Messiah, the Anointed One).
>
> —Romans 5:17

We receive God's grace (unmerited favor), overflowing grace, free gift of righteousness, right standing with God, and reign as kings with Jesus. That's us, people!

> So that, [just] as sin has reigned in death, [so] grace (His unearned and undeserved favor) might reign also through righteousness (right standing with God)

> which issues in eternal life through Jesus Christ (the Messiah, the Anointed One) our Lord.
>
> —Romans 5:21

We receive His grace, even though we don't deserve it and we can never earn it. We are righteous and have eternal life all because of Jesus. This is who we are!

> Are you ignorant of the fact that all of us who have been baptized into Christ Jesus were baptized into His death? We were buried therefore with Him by the baptism into death, so that just as Christ was raised from the dead by the glorious [power] of the Father, so we too might [habitually] live and behave in newness of life. For if we have become one with Him by sharing a death like His, we shall also be [one with Him in sharing] His resurrection [by a new life lived for God]. We know that our old (unrenewed) self was nailed to the cross with Him in order that [our] body [which is the instrument] of sin might be made ineffective and inactive for evil, that we might no longer be the slaves of sin. For when a man dies, he is freed (loosed, delivered) from [the power of] sin [among men]. Now if we have died with Christ, we believe that we shall also live with Him, because we know that Christ (the Anointed One), being once raised from the dead, will never die again; death no longer has power over Him. For by the death He died, He died to sin [ending His relation to it] once for all; and the life that He lives, He is living to God [in unbroken fellowship with Him]. Even so consider yourselves also dead to sin and your relation to it broken, but alive to God [living in unbroken fellowship with Him] in Christ Jesus.
>
> —Romans 6:3–11

So if your old self was buried with Christ, why are you sinning? We need to renew our minds with what God says about us now that we belong to Him. Through Him we have life, a life free from sin because He died for all sin and for all sinners. Do you realize we live in Him and He lives in us? We need to get our minds on what God says about us living dead to sin and that our relation to it is broken. We are living in Christ!

> For sin shall not [any longer] exert dominion over you, since now you are not under Law [as slaves], but under grace [as subjects of God's favor and mercy].
>
> —Romans 6:14

> And having been set free from sin, you have become the servants of righteousness (of conformity to the divine will in thought, purpose, and action).
>
> —Romans 6:18

So sin has no right to exert itself upon us because we who are in Christ are under God's grace. We have been set free from sin and are the servants of righteousness and do conform to the divine will in thought, purpose, and action! We need to tell ourselves this truth!

> For the wages which sin pays is death, but the [bountiful] free gift of God is eternal life through (in union with) Jesus Christ our Lord.
>
> —Romans 6:23

Tell yourself, "God gave me His bountiful free gift of grace through His Son, Jesus." Thank You, Lord, for eternal life with You!

Chapter 2

DEAD TO THE LAW

Likewise, my brethren, you have undergone death as to the Law through the [crucified] body of Christ, so that now you may belong to Another, to Him Who was raised from the dead in order that we may bear fruit for God.

—ROMANS 7:4

JESUS BEING CRUCIFIED has made us dead to the law. We belong to Him (God) who raised Jesus from the dead and we are now able and should bear fruit for God.

> O unhappy and pitiful and wretched man that I am! Who will release and deliver me from [the shackles of] this body of death? O thank God! [He will!] through Jesus Christ (the Anointed One) our Lord! So then indeed I, of myself with the mind and heart, serve the Law of God, but with the flesh the law of sin.
>
> —ROMANS 7:24–25

Who releases us from our old wretched self? God does! So one needs to ask a question of him or herself when sin wants to rule in you: Am I in God or in flesh? What is flesh, you ask? It is our human nature with all its frailty and/or passions. Our flesh does like to rule, but as one grows in Jesus Christ, God rules and we should recognize Him and say no to sin. Our flesh will be with us all the days we live on Earth, but does it rule or does God? We should be constantly reminding ourselves of who we are in Him.

And why should we do this?

> Therefore, [there is] now no condemnation (no adjudging guilty of wrong) for those who are in Christ Jesus, who live [and] walk not after the dictates of the flesh, but after the dictates of the Spirit. For the law of the Spirit of life [which is] in Christ Jesus [the law of our new being] has freed me from the law of sin and of death. For God has done what the Law could not do, [its power] being weakened by the flesh [the entire nature of man without the Holy Spirit]. Sending His own Son in the guise of sinful flesh and as an offering for sin, [God] condemned sin in the flesh [subdued, overcame, deprived it of its power over all who accept that sacrifice].
>
> —Romans 8:1–3

So who is guilty, in shame or condemned if they are in Christ Jesus? No one! We walk not in the flesh but in the Spirit, which is the law of our new being. Do you recognize you are a new being, perfected in Him? This living a new life is a day-by-day, and some days a moment-by-moment, perfecting. We are not our old self anymore. We are, as He says, a new creation (2 Cor. 5:17). We really need to recognize that Jesus did come and did subdue, overcome, and deprive sin of its power over all who accept Him as Savior.

> So then those who are living the life of the flesh [catering to the appetites and impulses of their carnal nature] cannot please or satisfy God, or be acceptable to Him. But you are not living the life of the flesh, you are living the life of the Spirit, if the [Holy] Spirit of God [really] dwells within you [directs and controls you]. But if anyone does not possess the [Holy]

> Spirit of Christ, he is none of His [he does not belong to Christ, is not truly a child of God]. But if Christ lives in you, [then although] your [natural] body is dead by reason of sin and guilt, the spirit is alive because of [the] righteousness [that He imputes to you]. And if the Spirit of Him Who raised up Jesus from the dead dwells in you, [then] He Who raised up Christ Jesus from the dead will also restore to life your mortal (short-lived, perishable) bodies through His Spirit Who dwells in you.
>
> —Romans 8:8–11

So who controls you? Your old carnal (sin) nature, or the new nature given by Jesus who lives in you? If the Spirit of God lives in us we should be controlled and led by the Spirit. God restored our spirit in us when we accepted Jesus. That takes us to a different level of communication—the level of the Spirit, not the flesh. So if the Spirit is leading you, who are you?

> For all who are led by the Spirit of God are sons of God.
>
> —Romans 8:14

> For those whom He foreknew [of whom He was aware and loved beforehand], He also destined from the beginning [foreordaining them] to be molded into the image of His Son [and share inwardly His likeness], that He might become the firstborn among many brethren. And those whom He thus foreordained, He also called; and those whom He called, He also justified (acquitted, made righteous, putting them into right standing with Himself). And those whom He justified, He also glorified [raising them to a heavenly dignity and condition or state of being].
>
> —Romans 8:29–30

Do you get this? He foreknew us; He destined us from the beginning and molded us into the image of His Son (His likeness). Foreordained, called, justified (just as if I'd never sinned), made righteous with God—and not only that, but He glorified us to a heavenly dignity, condition or state of being. With Jesus we are no longer dealing in the flesh unless we want to.

> Who shall bring any charge against God's elect [when it is] God Who justifies [that is, Who puts us in right relation to Himself? Who shall come forward and accuse or impeach those whom God has chosen? Will God, Who acquits us?] Who is there to condemn [us]? Will Christ Jesus (the Messiah), Who died, or rather Who was raised from the dead, Who is at the right hand of God actually pleading as He intercedes for us? Who shall ever separate us from Christ's love? Shall suffering and affliction and tribulation? Or calamity and distress? Or persecution or hunger or destitution or peril or sword? Even as it is written, For Thy sake we are put to death all the day long; we are regarded and counted as sheep for the slaughter. Yet amid all these things we are more than conquerors and gain a surpassing victory through Him Who loved us.
>
> —Romans 8:33–37

Do you recognize that He is so in you that even when all hell breaks loose it has no power over you? We need to look at battles as if they are already won, because they are already won! Jesus already paraded the devil and his cohorts around the heavenly realm showing Satan as a defeated foe (Col. 2:15).

> For I am persuaded beyond doubt (am sure) that neither death nor life, nor angels nor principalities, nor things impeding and threatening nor things to come,

> nor powers, nor height nor depth, nor anything else in all creation will be able to separate us from the love of God which is in Christ Jesus our Lord.
>
> —ROMANS 8:38–39

Are you fully persuaded? When you are totally sold out to God and do not move from what He has said, these things, though they happen, will not be able to drag you down and defeat you. *God loves you*!

> And [what if] He thus purposes to make known and show the wealth of His glory in [dealing with] the vessels [objects] of His mercy which He has prepared beforehand for glory, even including ourselves whom He has called, not only from among the Jews but also from among the Gentiles (heathen)? Just as He says in Hosea, Those who were not My people I will call My people, and her who was not beloved [I will call] My beloved. And it shall be that in the very place where it was said to them, You are not My people, they shall be called sons of the living God.
>
> —ROMANS 9:23–26

When we accepted Jesus we became a son or daughter of the living God! Recognize this and declare it!

> As it is written, Behold I am laying in Zion a Stone that will make men stumble, a Rock that will make them fall; but he who believes in Him [who adheres to, trusts in, and relies on Him] shall not be put to shame nor be disappointed in his expectations.
>
> —ROMANS 9:33

Therefore I believe on the Lord Jesus Christ and He is my Savior, so in Him I shall not be put to shame nor be disappointed in my expectations. Remember to line up your expectations with the Word!

> For Christ is the end of the Law [the limit at which it ceases to be, for the Law leads up to Him Who is the fulfillment of its types, and in Him the purpose which it was designed to accomplish is fulfilled. That is, the purpose of the Law is fulfilled in Him] as the means of righteousness (right relationship to God) for everyone who trusts in and adheres to and relies on Him.
>
> —Romans 10:4

When we accept Jesus as Savior we are put in right relationship with God. This is something I believe we as Christians so need to learn. All too often we keep ourselves locked in our old sin nature and do not realize that this is not who we are anymore. Jesus is the fulfillment of the Law. He is the One who was slain from the foundation of the earth (Rev. 13:8), once for all, sin and sinners (Heb. 7:26–27; 10:10; 1 Pet. 3:18). He didn't just die for the sins of our past; He also paid the price for the sins we may do today or tomorrow. He died once for all sin and for all sinners. The question is, do you know that since the day you accepted Jesus as your Savior, God no longer looks at you as a sinner? He looks at you as a son. The only way you lose that sonship is by rejecting Him, "by speaking abusively against or maliciously misrepresenting the Holy Spirit" (Mark 3:29). This is done by saying God did something when you know it was the devil or God does do something and you give credit to the devil.

> Because if you acknowledge and confess with your lips that Jesus is Lord and in your heart believe (adhere to, trust in, and rely on the truth) that God raised Him from the dead, you will be saved. For with the heart a person believes (adheres to, trusts in, and relies on Christ) and so is justified (declared righteous, acceptable to God), and with the mouth he confesses (declares openly and speaks out freely his

> faith) and confirms [his] salvation. The Scripture says, No man who believes in Him [who adheres to, relies on, and trusts in Him] will [ever] be put to shame or be disappointed...For everyone who calls upon the name of the Lord [invoking Him as Lord] will be saved.
>
> —Romans 10:9–11, 13

Believe, repent, acknowledge Him, and be declared righteous, saved, never put to shame or disappointed. I'd say that's a pretty good deal!

> For God's gifts and His call are irrevocable. [He never withdraws them when once they are given, and He does not change His mind about those to whom He gives His grace or to whom He sends His call].
>
> —Romans 11:29

The world cannot beat this gift from God. Grace is irrevocable and He does not change His mind.

> Oh, the depth of the riches and wisdom and knowledge of God! How unfathomable (inscrutable, unsearchable) are His judgments (His decisions)! And how untraceable (mysterious, undiscoverable) are His ways (His methods, His paths)! For who has known the mind of the Lord and who has understood His thoughts, or who has [ever] been His counselor? Or who has first given God anything that he might be paid back or that he could recompense? For from Him and through Him and to Him are all things. [For all things originate with Him and come from Him; all things live through Him and all things center in and tend to consummate and to end in Him.] To Him be glory forever! Amen (so be it).
>
> —Romans 11:33–36

Paul is asking a question in these verses that quite often people misinterpret. I have heard preachers say that we can't know the mind of God, but one needs to keep reading…

> Do not be conformed to this world (this age), [fashioned after and adapted to its external, superficial customs], but be transformed (changed) by the [entire] renewal of your mind [by its new ideals and its new attitude], so that you may prove [for yourselves] what is the good and acceptable and perfect will of God, even the thing which is good and acceptable and perfect [in His sight for you].
>
> —Romans 12:2

According to this scripture we can know the mind of God. Furthermore, He wants us to know what He thinks and what He wants us to do. We just have to make the choice to transform into His way of being, thinking, moving. And it is not hard to do this because He has given us the Word to speak to bring Him in us to pass.

Chapter 3

THE BODY OF CHRIST

So we, numerous as we are, are one body in Christ (the Messiah) and individually we are parts one of another [mutually dependent on one another].

—Romans 12:5

All believers are the body of Christ. That includes all churches that have believers in them. The "church" as a whole has not recognized that believers are everywhere. Quite often it has been taught that only our "church" is the one that is going to heaven. Oh, that is such a sad place to be because it is a lie. God says, "*all who call upon Me will be saved.*" That includes someone in a place we may not think is teaching what we believe. If that person calls on the name of the Lord, the Lord will hear and answer and save. Thank You, Jesus!

Romans 12:11 is a good scripture to pray over oneself:

> [Lord, help me to] Never lag in zeal and in earnest endeavor; [help me] be aglow and burning with the Spirit, serving [You] the Lord.

Romans 13:14—pray this too!

> [Lord, I] But clothe [myself] with the Lord Jesus Christ (the Messiah), and make no provision for

> [indulging] the flesh [I] [put a stop to thinking about the evil cravings of (my) physical nature] to [gratify its] desires (lusts).

Romans 15:5–6; pray this as well:

> Now may the God Who gives the power of patient endurance (steadfastness) and Who supplies encouragement, grant you to live in such mutual harmony and such full sympathy with one another, in accord with Christ Jesus, that together you may [unanimously] with united hearts and one voice, praise and glorify the God and Father of our Lord Jesus Christ (the Messiah).

God gives power of patient endurance, supplies encouragement, and grants mutual harmony and full sympathy so we can live with united hearts, and with one voice praise and glorify God and His Son, Jesus. This is who we are in Him!

> In Christ Jesus, then, I have legitimate reason to glory (exult) in my work for God [in what through Christ Jesus I have accomplished concerning the things of God].
>
> —Romans 15:17

In Christ I have a legitimate reason to glory for what I have done and been called to do for God. Wow!

> To the church (assembly) of God which is in Corinth, to those consecrated and purified and made holy in Christ Jesus, [who are] selected and called to be saints (God's people), together with all those who in any place call upon and give honor to the name of our Lord Jesus Christ, both their Lord and ours.
>
> —1 Corinthians 1:2

Who is the church? The church is any person who believes on the Lord Jesus Christ. In that believing it is more than just knowing about Him. It is a personal relationship with Him. So when we accept Him as Savior and make Him Lord we are consecrated, purified, and made holy, and we've been selected and called His people. This means all those who call on His name, not just those who attend the "church" building we attend. Wow! How many of us think of ourselves in this manner?

> I thank my God at all times for you because of the grace (the favor and spiritual blessing) of God which was bestowed on you in Christ Jesus.
>
> —1 Corinthians 1:4

> [So] that in Him in every respect you were enriched, in full power and readiness of speech [to speak of your faith] and complete knowledge and illumination [to give you full insight into its meaning]. In this way [our] witnessing concerning Christ (the Messiah) was so confirmed and established and made sure in you.
>
> —1 Corinthians 1:5–6

We have been bestowed with grace, favor, and spiritual blessing from God through Jesus. We are enriched with full power and readiness of speech to be able to tell what Jesus in us has done for us. We've been given full knowledge and illumination of the meaning of us being in Christ. Our witness is confirmed and established!

> God is faithful (reliable, trustworthy, and therefore ever true to His promise, and He can be depended on); By Him you were called into companionship and participation with His Son, Jesus Christ our Lord.
>
> —1 Corinthians 1:9

Who called you into companionship and participation with His Son, Jesus Christ? God the Father did. That means we are companions with Jesus and participate in everything the Father granted Him (John 14:12), including be mocked, scorned, and ridiculed. But remember He overcame all this (John 16:33). And we overcome by the blood of the Lamb and the word of our testimony (Rev. 12:11).

> But it is from Him that you have your life in Christ Jesus, Whom God made our Wisdom from God, [revealed to us a knowledge of the divine plan of salvation previously hidden, manifesting itself as] our Righteousness [thus making us upright and putting us in right standing with God], and our Consecration [making us pure and holy], and our Redemption [providing our ransom from eternal penalty for sin].
>
> —1 Corinthians 1:30

Do you recognize what God did for us through Jesus? Jesus in us, His wisdom (revealed knowledge), righteousness (making us upright and in right standing with God), consecration (making us pure and holy), and our redemption (He paid the penalty for all our sins, past, present, and future). Do you think of yourself as wise? God says to ask wisdom of Him and He will liberally give it (James 1:5). Do you look at yourself as God says of you that you are in right standing with Him? Do you know you have been consecrated (made pure and holy)? Do you really know you were redeemed? God looks at us in these ways as soon as we accept Jesus as Savior and He doesn't stop looking at us in these ways just because we mess up. However if we continue thinking we can sin and it doesn't matter, remember then we aren't in Jesus (1 John 3:6–10).

Pray these verses. Read 1 Corinthians 2:4–5 as it is written in the Bible before praying out what I wrote:

Lord, my words and message may not be set forth in persuasive (enticing and plausible) words of wisdom, but they are demonstration of the [Holy] Spirit and power [a proof by the Spirit and power of God, operating on me and stirring in the minds of my hearers the most holy emotions and thus persuading them]. So that their faith might not rest in the wisdom of men (human philosophy), but in the power of God.

But rather what we are setting forth is a wisdom of God once hidden [from the human understanding] and now revealed to us by God—[that wisdom] which God devised and decreed before the ages for our glorification [to lift us into the glory of His presence]. None of the rulers of this age or world perceived and recognized and understood this, for if they had, they would never have crucified the Lord of glory. But, on the contrary, as the Scripture says, What eye has not seen and ear has not heard and has not entered into the heart of man, [all that] God has prepared (made and keeps ready) for those who love Him [who hold Him in affectionate reverence, promptly obeying Him and gratefully recognizing the benefits He has bestowed.] Yet to us God has unveiled and revealed them by and through His Spirit, for the [Holy] Spirit searches diligently, exploring and examining everything, even sounding the profound and bottomless things of God [the divine counsels and things hidden and beyond man's scrutiny]. For what person perceives (knows and understands) what passes through a man's thoughts except the man's own spirit within him? Just so no one discerns (comes to know and comprehend) the thoughts of God except the Spirit of God. Now we have not received the spirit [that belongs to] the world, but the [Holy] Spirit Who is

> from God, [given to us] that we might realize and comprehend and appreciate the gifts [of divine favor and blessings so freely and lavishly] bestowed on us by God. And we are setting these truths forth in words not taught by human wisdom, but taught by the [Holy] Spirit, combining and interpreting spiritual truths with spiritual language [to those who possess the Holy Spirit].
>
> —1 CORINTHIANS 2:7–13

How do all the gifts come to us? By the Spirit! We just have to recognize that they are in us and are fully operational. As we seek the Lord in any situation we are faced with, the Spirit will teach us what God reveals and we will succeed in whatever endeavor we are placed in. All these gifts are the attributes of God, His nature in us.

> For who has known or understood the mind (the counsels and purposes) of the Lord so as to guide and instruct Him and give Him knowledge? But we have the mind of Christ (the Messiah) and do hold the thoughts (feelings and purposes) of His heart.
>
> —1 CORINTHIANS 2:16

Christ in us. His mind, His will, His thoughts, feelings, and purposes. When we read the scripture in Isaiah that states, "My thoughts are not your thoughts, and My ways are not your ways" (Isa. 55:8), we need to understand that when God said this it was spoken in the old covenant, when only the prophets and some others heard from God when God had something to say. But now after Jesus we have a new covenant (Luke 22:20) and therefore all have access to hear and know what God is saying.

> Do you not discern and understand that you [the whole church at Corinth] are God's temple (His sanctuary), and that God's Spirit has His permanent

> dwelling in you [to be home in you, collectively as a church and also individually]?
>
> —1 Corinthians 3:16

> And you are Christ's and Christ is God's.
>
> —1 Corinthians 3:23

So I speak forth that I am the temple of God. His Spirit lives permanently in me—not only me, but all believers. I belong to and am in Christ and Christ is in God.

> So then, let us [apostles] be looked upon as ministering servants of Christ and stewards (trustees) of the mysteries (the secret purposes) of God.
>
> —1 Corinthians 4:1

Not only the apostles but all who are in Christ are ministering servants of Christ and stewards of the mysteries of God.

> Yet for us there is [only] one God, the Father, Who is the Source of all things, and for Whom we [have life], and one Lord, Jesus Christ, through and by Whom are all things and through and by Whom we [ourselves exist].
>
> —1 Corinthians 8:6

One God, our Source for all things, in whom we have life; and Jesus, in whom all things, including us, exist.

> Therefore I want you to understand that no one speaking under the power and influence of the [Holy] Spirit of God can [ever] say, Jesus be cursed! And no one can [really] say Jesus is [my] Lord, except by and under the power and influence of the Holy Spirit.
>
> —1 Corinthians 12:3

> But to each one is given the manifestation of the [Holy] Spirit [the evidence, the spiritual illumination of the Spirit] for good and profit.
>
> —1 Corinthians 12:7

> For just as the body is a unity and yet has many parts, and all the parts, though many, form [only] one body, so it is with Christ (the Messiah, the Anointed One).
>
> —1 Corinthians 12:12

> Now you [collectively] are Christ's body and [individually] you are members of it, each part severally and distinct [each with his own place and function].
>
> —1 Corinthians 12:27

We are all the body of Christ and we are influenced by the Holy Spirit for our good and profit. The body of Christ has many parts collectively and individually. We all have our own place and function!

Chapter 4

ALIVE IN CHRIST

For just as [because of their union of nature] in Adam all people die, so also [by virtue of their union of nature] shall all in Christ be made alive.

—1 Corinthians 15:22

WOW! MY AND your union with Christ makes us alive!

For this perishable [part of us] must put on the imperishable [nature], and this mortal [part of us, this nature that is capable of dying] must put on immortality (freedom from death). And when this perishable puts on the imperishable and this that was capable of dying puts on freedom from death, then shall be fulfilled the Scripture that says, Death is swallowed up (utterly vanquished forever) in and unto victory. O death, where is your victory? O death, where is your sting? Now sin is the sting of death, and sin exercises its power [upon the soul] through [the abuse of] the Law. But thanks be to God, Who gives us the victory [making us conquerors] through our Lord Jesus Christ. Therefore, my beloved brethren, be firm (steadfast), immovable, always abounding in the work of the Lord [always being superior, excelling,

> doing more than enough in the service of the Lord], knowing and being continually aware that your labor in the Lord is not futile [it is never wasted or to no purpose].
>
> —1 CORINTHIANS 15:53–58

We put on imperishable, we are free from death (true death is total separation from God forever). We have victory through Jesus so we can do all that God wants us to do and do it well. When we do something well and we know God told us to do it, it makes Him look good.

> For just as Christ's [own] sufferings fall to our lot [as they overflow upon His disciples, and we share and experience them] abundantly, so through Christ comfort (consolation and encouragement) is also [shared and experienced] abundantly by us....For as many as are the promises of God, they all find their Yes [answer] in Him [Christ]. For this reason we also utter the Amen (so be it) to God through Him [in His Person and by His agency] to the glory of God.
>
> —2 CORINTHIANS 1:5, 20

Yes, we are going to have our share of suffering, but Christ is so in us that we will always be comforted and encouraged and will be supplied abundantly for whatever experience we are going through. All God has promised us is ours through Jesus! Do you get this? And all of it will glorify God!

> But thanks be to God, Who in Christ always leads us in triumph [as trophies of Christ's victory] and through us spreads and makes evident the fragrance of the knowledge of God everywhere.
>
> —2 CORINTHIANS 2:14

Yes! This is Christ in us! We are His visible victory and we spread the good news of God everywhere.

> You show and make obvious that you are a letter from Christ delivered by us, not written with ink but with [the] Spirit of [the] living God, not on tablets of stone but on tablets of human hearts. Such is the reliance and confidence that we have through Christ toward and with reference to God. Not that we are fit (qualified and sufficient in ability) of ourselves to form personal judgments or to claim or count anything as coming from us, but our power and ability and sufficiency are from God. [It is He] Who has qualified us [making us to be fit and worthy and sufficient] as ministers and dispensers of a new covenant [of salvation through Christ], not [ministers] of the letter (of legally written code) but of the Spirit; for the code [of the Law] kills, but the [Holy] Spirit makes alive.
>
> —2 CORINTHIANS 3:3–6

When we do things right we make God look good! We need to remember it is not our abilities but God's. He has qualified us by Christ and His new covenant and His Spirit in us makes us alive!

> But whenever a person turns [in repentance] to the Lord, the veil is stripped off and taken away. Now the Lord is the Spirit, and where the Spirit of the Lord is, there is liberty (emancipation from bondage, freedom). And all of us, as with unveiled face, [because we] continued to behold [in the Word of God] as in a mirror the glory of the Lord, are constantly being transfigured into His *very own* image in ever increasing splendor and from one degree of glory to another; [for this comes] from the Lord [Who is] the Spirit.
>
> —2 CORINTHIANS 3:16–18

Liberated, set free from bondage, behold the Word of God, see the glory of the Lord and are transfigured into His *very own* image. This is what Keith Moore taught about going from glory to glory. It is when God shows us something in us that needs to be dealt with or when He would like to teach us something new. When we learn what it is He is removing from us and release it to Him to remove, or embrace the new thing He is teaching us, we go from one level of glory to another. That's the going from glory to glory. We should be growing in the Lord and changing to look so like Jesus that God the Father sees only Him in us!

> Therefore if any person is [ingrafted] in Christ (the Messiah) he is a new creation (a new creature altogether); the old [previous moral and spiritual condition] has passed away. Behold, the fresh and new has come! But all things are from God, Who through Jesus Christ reconciled us to Himself [received us into favor, brought us into harmony with Himself] and gave to us the ministry of reconciliation [that by word and deed we might aim to bring others into harmony with Him].
>
> —2 Corinthians 5:17–18

Do you realize you are a new creation? Your old self has been removed. Yes we still have to battle our flesh; but when we start speaking what God says about us, that old flesh doesn't stand a chance to keep us in our old bondage! And our mind needs to hear this! Say out loud what God says you are, not what you think you are. Get over the sin you just did, repent, and receive God's forgiveness and don't drag yourself down into the gutter again. Tell the devil and all his cohorts, "This is what God says I am in Him..."

> So we are Christ's ambassadors, God making His appeal as it were through us. We [as Christ's personal representatives] beg you for His sake to lay hold of the divine favor [now offered you] and be reconciled

> to God. For our sake He made Christ [virtually] to be sin Who knew no sin, so that in and through Him we might become [endued with, viewed as being in, and examples of] the righteousness of God [what we ought to be, approved and acceptable and in right relationship with Him, by His goodness].
>
> —2 Corinthians 5:20–21

Christ's ambassadors; God speaking through us to draw others to Him; endued with, viewed as being in and an example of what the righteousness of God looks like; approved, accepted and in right relationship with Him, all because of His goodness. This is who we are in Him!

> And God is able to make all grace (every favor and earthly blessing) come to you in abundance, so that you may always and under all circumstances and whatever the need be self-sufficient [possessing enough to require no aid or support and furnished in abundance for every good work and charitable donation]. As it is written, He [the benevolent person] scatters abroad; he gives to the poor; His deeds of justice and goodness and kindness and benevolence will go on and endure forever! And [God] Who provides seed for the sower and bread for eating will also provide and multiply your [resources for] sowing and increase the fruits of your righteousness [which manifests itself in active goodness, kindness, and charity]. Thus you will be enriched in all things and in every way, so that you can be generous, and [your generosity as it is] administered by us will bring forth thanksgiving to God.
>
> —2 Corinthians 9:8–11

This is who God says we are, and what will happen for us and through us if we live in Him!

> For though we walk (live) in the flesh, we are not carrying on our warfare according to the flesh and using mere human weapons. For the weapons of our warfare are not physical [weapons of flesh and blood], but they are mighty before God for the overthrow and destruction of strongholds. [Inasmuch as we] refute arguments and theories and reasonings and every proud and lofty thing that sets itself up against the [true] knowledge of God; and we lead every thought and purpose away captive into the obedience of Christ (the Messiah, the Anointed One).
>
> —2 Corinthians 10:3–5

So what are your thoughts telling you about yourself? Do they line up with what God says about you?

> Look at [this obvious fact] which is before your eyes. If anyone is confident that he is Christ's, let him reflect and remind himself that even as he is Christ's, so too are we.
>
> —2 Corinthians 10:7

We are supposed to remind ourselves that we are Christ's. Others too belong to Christ and sometimes we need to remind them. Look at Psalm 107:2: "Let the redeemed of the Lord say so, whom He has delivered from the hand of the adversary." Say SO! Speak it out that you belong to Him!

> However, let him who boasts and glories boast and glory in the Lord. For [it is] not [the man] who praises and commends himself who is approved and accepted, but [it is the person] whom the Lord accredits and commends.
>
> —2 Corinthians 10:17–18

This is certainly correct; we don't lift ourselves up and boast in what we have done, we boast in what the Lord has done and the Lord does the rest, accrediting and commending. God promotes.

> For I am zealous for you with a godly eagerness and a divine jealousy, for I have betrothed you to one Husband, to present you as a chaste virgin to Christ.
>
> —2 Corinthians 11:2

Have you ever thought of yourself as a chaste virgin betrothed to God? Well you are!

> As the truth of Christ is in me, this my boast [of independence] shall not be debarred (silenced or checked) in the regions of Achaia (most of Greece).
>
> —2 Corinthians 11:10

If the truth of Christ is in Paul is it not in you also?

> But He said to me, My grace (My favor and loving-kindness and mercy) is enough for you [sufficient against any danger and enables you to bear the trouble manfully]; for My strength and power are made perfect (fulfilled and completed) and show themselves most effective in [your] weakness. Therefore, I will all the more gladly glory in my weaknesses and infirmities, that the strength and power of Christ (the Messiah) may rest (yes, may pitch a tent over and dwell) upon me!
>
> —2 Corinthians 12:9

God's grace dwells in me and it is enough for every situation; His strength is made perfect in my weakness and I too will glory in Christ's power and strength resting upon me! This is who I am in Him.

> Examine and test and evaluate your own selves to see whether you are holding to your faith and showing

> the proper fruits of it. Test and prove yourselves [not Christ]. Do you not yourselves realize and know [thoroughly by an ever-increasing experience] that Jesus Christ is in you—unless you are [counterfeits] disapproved on trial and rejected? But I hope you will recognize and know that we are not disapproved on trial and rejected.
>
> —2 Corinthians 13:5–6

> The grace (favor and spiritual blessing) of the Lord Jesus Christ and the love of God and the presence and fellowship (that communion and sharing together, and participation) in the Holy Spirit be with you all. Amen (*so be it*).
>
> —2 Corinthians 13:14

Examine yourselves; really look to see what you are saying about yourself. Do you really believe that Christ lives in you? I heard Joyce Meyer make this statement about being born again. She said that when you are born again your new spirit comes right down into your old flesh and as you grow in the Lord, your old self-flesh should be less and less able to rise as Christ grows in you. That is the putting the flesh to death daily until it becomes such a habit that soon your flesh can't even rise up. I love how Paul ended this chapter by praying the grace, presence, and fellowship of Christ in us as well as the Holy Spirit. (The Lord has just taught me something I'd never really recognized about the Holy Spirit, but I'll study and write that out at a later time.)

> Grace and spiritual blessing be to you and [soul] peace from God the Father and our Lord Jesus Christ (the Messiah).
>
> —Galatians 1:3

We receive grace, spiritual blessing, and peace from God and Jesus. Do you really know this is promised in Him?

Chapter 5

JUSTIFIED BY FAITH

Yet we know that a man is justified or reckoned righteous and in right standing with God not by works of the Law, but [only] through faith and [absolute] reliance on and adherence to and trust in Jesus Christ (the Messiah, the Anointed One). [Therefore] even we [ourselves] have believed on Christ Jesus, in order to be justified by faith in Christ and not by works of the Law [for we cannot be justified by any observance of the ritual of the Law given by Moses], because by keeping legal rituals and by works no human being can ever be justified (declared righteous and put in right standing with God).... I have been crucified with Christ [in Him I have shared His crucifixion]; it is no longer I who live, but Christ (the Messiah) lives in me; and the life I now live in the body I live by faith in (by adherence to and reliance on and complete trust in) the Son of God, Who loved me and gave Himself up for me.

—*Galatians 2:16, 20*

Faith, not works, justifies me. I have been and am crucified with Christ. I no longer live; but Christ lives in me (John 17:23); the new me lives! I just have to choose to let the new me live and put to death the old me. Stop talking the old and speak what Christ says about me now that I live by faith in Him!

> Now it is evident that no person is justified (declared righteous and brought into right standing with God) through the Law, for the Scripture says, The man in right standing with God [the just, the righteous] shall live by and out of faith and he who through and by faith is declared righteous and in right standing with God shall live.
>
> —GALATIANS 3:11

We are justified by faith and made to be in right standing with God and by our faith and right standing with God we shall live. Wow! That's a cool way to live!

> Christ purchased our freedom [redeeming us] from the curse (doom) of the Law [and its condemnation] by [Himself] becoming a curse for us, for it is written [in the Scriptures], Cursed is everyone who hangs on a tree (is crucified).
>
> —GALATIANS 3:13

Jesus purchased our freedom and redeemed us from the curse. Do you tell yourself you're free and redeemed in Him?

> But the Scriptures [picture all mankind as sinners] shut up and imprisoned by sin, so that [the inheritance, blessing] which was promised through faith in Jesus Christ (the Messiah) might be given (released, delivered, and committed) to [all] those who believe [who adhere to and trust in and rely on Him].
>
> —GALATIANS 3:22

Believe in Jesus! Cry out to Him for salvation! If we do, we can be assured that we will be released and delivered from all sin. Jesus is committed to our transformation.

> For in Christ Jesus you are all sons of God through faith. For as many [of you] as were baptized into Christ [into a spiritual union and communion with Christ, the Anointed One, the Messiah] have put on (clothed yourselves with) Christ...And if you belong to Christ [are in Him Who is Abraham's Seed], then you are Abraham's offspring and [spiritual] heirs according to promise.
>
> —Galatians 3:26–27, 29

I am a son of God. I am baptized into Christ and He has clothed me with Himself. Remember Christ means the Anointed One or Anointing. So I am anointed with Him. I am in Christ and therefore I am an heir according to the promise.

> But when the proper time had fully come, God sent His Son, born of a woman, born subject to [the regulations of] the Law, to purchase the freedom of (to ransom, to redeem, to atone for) those who were subject to the Law, that we might be adopted and have sonship conferred upon us [and be recognized as God's sons]. And because you [really] are [His] sons, God has sent the [Holy] Spirit of His Son into our hearts, crying, Abba (Father)! Father! Therefore, you are no longer a slave (bond servant) but a son; and if a son, then [it follows that you are] an heir by the aid of God, through Christ.
>
> —Galatians 4:4–7

I am a son or daughter through Christ! I am an heir! Thank You, Father God!

> So, brethren, we [who are born again] are not children of a slave woman [the natural], but of the free [the supernatural].
>
> —Galatians 4:31

One cannot read verse 31 without reading on into...

> In [this] freedom Christ has made us free [and completely liberated us]; stand fast then, and do not be hampered and held ensnared and submit again to a yoke of slavery [which you have once put off].
>
> —Galatians 5:1

We are free! Liberated completely! Do you really know this? Ask God to renew your mind to this way of thinking! Don't go back into the old way of thinking about yourself!

> For we, [not relying on the Law but] through the [Holy] Spirit's [help], by faith anticipate and wait for the blessing and good for which our righteousness and right standing with God [our conformity to His will in purpose, thought, and action, causes us] to hope. For [if we are] in Christ Jesus, neither circumcision nor uncircumcision counts for anything, but only faith activated and energized and expressed and working through love.
>
> —Galatians 5:5–6

Only faith counts. We should be conformed to His will in purpose, thought, and action. We should purpose what He says, think what He says, and act accordingly to what He says—all done in like-mindedness with the Word. So what are you thinking, speaking, and doing? Is what you are thinking, speaking, or doing in accordance with what the Word says? Is it faith or is it unbelief?

> But the fruit of the [Holy] Spirit [the work which His presence within accomplishes] is love, joy (gladness), peace, patience (an even temper, forbearance), kindness, goodness (benevolence), faithfulness, gentleness (meekness, humility), self-control (self-restraint, continence). Against such things there is no law [that can

> bring a charge]. And those who belong to Christ Jesus (the Messiah) have crucified the flesh (the godless human nature) with its passions and appetites and desires. If we live by the [Holy] Spirit, let us also walk by the Spirit. [If by the Holy Spirit we have our life in God, let us go forward walking in line, our conduct controlled by the Spirit.] Let us not become vainglorious and self-conceited, competitive and challenging and provoking and irritating to one another, envying and being jealous of one another.
>
> —Galatians 5:22–26

Let's look at this closely. The fruit of the Holy Spirit is His (God's) presence within us. All these fruits are attributes of God and since He lives in us these fruits are in us and operational. We should have crucified the flesh and some days still have to crucify it. But the thing is, do you know you have authority in Him to tell your flesh, "No more ruling me"? If we truly walk in the Spirit we are controlled by the Spirit; and if we are controlled by the Spirit the flesh hasn't a chance to resurrect itself. All that vainglorious, self-conceited competition and challenging, provoking, and irritating is of the flesh. Now what do you want pouring out of you? We will spend eternity finding out all the attributes of God but it is a wonderful thing to begin understanding who He is in us now and begin working in Him and with Him, agreeing with what He says we are.

> The grace (spiritual favor, blessing) of our Lord Jesus Christ (the Anointed One, the Messiah) be with your spirit, brethren. Amen (so be it).
>
> —Galatians 6:18

We should pray this over ourselves—not just pray it, but believe this about who we are in Christ!

May blessing (praise, laudation, and eulogy) be to the God and Father of our Lord Jesus Christ (the Messiah) Who has blessed us *in Christ* with every spiritual (given by the Holy Spirit) blessing in the heavenly realm! Even as [in His love] He chose us [actually picked us out for Himself as His own] in Christ before the foundation of the world, that we should be holy (consecrated and set apart for Him) and blameless in His sight, even above reproach, before Him in love. For He foreordained us (destined us, planned in love for us) to be adopted (revealed) as His own children through Jesus Christ, in accordance with the purpose of His will (because it pleased Him and was His kind intent)—[So that we might be] to the praise and the commendation of His glorious grace (favor and mercy), which He so freely bestowed on us in the Beloved.

In Him we have redemption (deliverance and salvation) through His blood, the remission (forgiveness) of our offenses (shortcomings and trespasses), in accordance with the riches and the generosity of His gracious favor, which He lavished upon us in every kind of wisdom and understanding (practical insight and prudence), making known to us the mystery (secret) of His will (of His plan, of His purpose). [And it is this:] In accordance with His good pleasure (His merciful intention) which He had previously purposed and set forth in Him, [He planned] for the maturity of the times and the climax of the ages to unify all things and head them up and consummate them in Christ, [both] things in heaven and things on the earth.

—Ephesians 1:3–10

In Him we also were made [God's] heritage (portion) and we obtained an inheritance; for we had been foreordained (chosen and appointed beforehand) in accordance with His purpose, Who works out everything in agreement with the counsel and design of His [own] will, so that we who first hoped in Christ [who first put our confidence in Him have been destined and appointed to] live for the praise of His glory! In Him you also who have heard the Word of Truth, the glad tidings (Gospel) of your salvation, and have believed in and adhered to and relied on Him, were stamped with the seal of the long-promised Holy Spirit. That [Spirit] is the guarantee of our inheritance [the firstfruits, the pledge and foretaste, the down payment on our heritage], in anticipation of its full redemption and our acquiring [complete] possession of it—to the praise of His glory.

—Ephesians 1:11–14

[For I always pray to] the God of our Lord Jesus Christ, the Father of glory, that He may grant you a spirit of wisdom and revelation [of insight into mysteries and secrets] in the [deep and intimate] knowledge of Him, by having the eyes of your heart flooded with light, so that you can know and understand the hope to which He has called you, and how rich is His glorious inheritance in the saints (His set-apart ones), and [so that you can know and understand] what is the immeasurable and unlimited and surpassing greatness of His power in and for us who believe, as demonstrated in the working of His mighty strength, which He exerted in Christ when He raised Him from the dead and seated Him at His [own] right hand in the heavenly [places], far above all rule and authority and power and dominion and every name that is named [above every title that can be conferred], not only in this age and in this world, but also in the age and the world which are to come. And He has put all things

> under His feet and has appointed Him the universal and supreme Head of the church [a headship exercised throughout the church], which is His body, the fullness of Him Who fills all in all [for in that body lives the full measure of Him Who makes everything complete, and Who fills everything everywhere with Himself].
>
> —Ephesians 1:17–23

This entire chapter is powerful to pray over oneself. This chapter says who we are in Christ and what He desires to place in us, and in whose authority we stand. God wants to place everything He has in you so that you operate in His fullness! Pray these words over yourself and believe it is so. However, do not just pray this over yourself; also pray it over your loved ones. The Word works! When I did this my whole world changed! The Word became alive!

> Even when we were dead (slain) by [our own] shortcomings and trespasses, He made us alive together in fellowship and in union with Christ; [He gave us the very life of Christ Himself, the same new life with which He quickened Him, for] it is by grace (His favor and mercy which you did not deserve) that you are saved (delivered from judgment and made partakers of Christ's salvation). And He raised us up together with Him and made us sit down together [giving us joint seating with Him] in the heavenly sphere [by virtue of our being] in Christ Jesus (the Messiah, the Anointed One). He did this that He might clearly demonstrate through the ages to come the immeasurable (limitless, surpassing) riches of His free grace (His unmerited favor) in [His] kindness and goodness of heart toward us in Christ Jesus. For it is by free grace (God's unmerited favor) that you are saved (delivered from judgment and made

> partakers of Christ's salvation) through [your] faith. And this [salvation] is not of yourselves [of your own doing, it came not of your own striving], but it is the gift of God.
>
> —Ephesians 2:5–8

He gave us the very life of Christ, that is Jesus in us! We are jointly seated with Him in the heavenly sphere, all because He loved us so and made His grace available to and for us.

> For we are God's [own] handiwork (His workmanship), recreated in Christ Jesus, [born anew] that we may do those good works which God predestined (planned beforehand) for us [taking paths which He prepared ahead of time], that we should walk in them [living the good life which He prearranged and made ready for us to live].
>
> —Ephesians 2:10

Wow! Recreated, predestined, good works, things prepared for us, and prearranged for a good life for us to live. That does not sound like how so many of us are living. But since God says this is for us we need to say what He says!

> But now in Christ Jesus, you who once were [so] far away, through (by, in) the blood of Christ have been brought near.
>
> —Ephesians 2:13

Thank You, Lord, for bringing me near to You! Thank You for Your blood!

> You are built upon the foundation of the apostles and prophets with Christ Jesus Himself the chief Cornerstone. In Him the whole structure is joined (bound, welded) together harmoniously, and it continues to rise (grow, increase) into a holy temple in

> the Lord [a sanctuary dedicated, consecrated, and sacred to the presence of the Lord]. In Him [and in fellowship with one another] you yourselves also are being built up [into this structure], with the rest, to form a fixed abode (dwelling place) of God in (by, through) the Spirit.
>
> —Ephesians 2:20–22

Built on the foundation of the apostles and prophets with Jesus the chief Cornerstone. Joined in harmony into a holy temple in the Lord, dedicated, consecrated to the presence of the Lord. In Him being built up to form a dwelling place of God by His Spirit. This is us in Him!

> When you read this you can understand my insight into the mystery of Christ:
>
> —Ephesians 3:4

When you read the Word you can understand the mystery of Christ is Christ in you.

> Also to enlighten all men and make plain to them what is the plan [regarding the Gentiles and providing for the salvation of all men] of the mystery kept hidden through the ages and concealed until now in [the mind of] God Who created all things *by Christ Jesus.* [The purpose is] that through the church the complicated, many-sided wisdom of God in all its infinite variety and innumerable aspects might now be made known to the angelic rulers and authorities (principalities and powers) in the heavenly sphere.
>
> —Ephesians 3:9–10

Wow, Gentiles can be saved! That means us. And look at the purpose God has. So God's wisdom, in all His aspects—or another way of saying this could be "all His attributes"—can be made known to the angelic rulers and authorities. And just whom do you think God has that come through? This is why salvation is given to all men. Because God desires for all of us to have all of Him so that those angelic rulers and authorities will know we are His sons.

> In Whom, because of our faith in Him, we dare to have the boldness (courage and confidence) of free access (an unreserved approach to God with freedom and without fear). So I ask you not to lose heart [not to faint or become despondent through fear] at what I am suffering in your behalf. [Rather glory in it] for it is an honor to you. For this reason [seeing the greatness of this plan by which you are built together in Christ], I bow my knees before the Father *of our Lord Jesus Christ.* For Whom every father in heaven and on earth is named [that Father from Whom all fatherhood takes its title and derives its name]. May He grant you out of the rich treasury of His glory to be strengthened and reinforced with mighty power in the inner man by the [Holy] Spirit [Himself indwelling your innermost being and personality]. May Christ through your faith [actually] dwell (settle down, abide, make His permanent home) in your hearts! May you be rooted deep in love and founded securely on love, that you may have the power and be strong to apprehend and grasp with all the saints [God's devoted people, the experience of that love] what is the breadth and length and height and depth [of it]; [That you may really come] to know [practically, through experience for yourselves] the love of Christ, which far surpasses mere knowledge [without experience]; that you may be filled [through all your being] unto all the fullness of God [may have the richest measure of the divine Presence, and become a body wholly filled and flooded with God Himself]! Now to Him Who, by (in consequence of) the [action

> of His] power that is at work within us, is able to [carry out His purpose and] do superabundantly, far over and above all that we [dare] ask or think [infinitely beyond our highest prayers, desires, thoughts, hopes, or dreams]—To Him be glory in the church and in Christ Jesus throughout all generations forever and ever. Amen (so be it).
>
> —Ephesians 3:12–21

These are powerful words to pray over yourself. I did this (and continue to do it) and man, did Jesus become real to me! I have learned more of Him and who He is in me since beginning to read and pray these scriptures. The Word changes your thoughts about who you are, and as Hebrews 4:12 says, "it is sharper than any two-edged sword." It cuts out untruth. All I can say is when I began praying this word over myself I changed. God became more real to me than ever before; His Word became alive! And He is filling me with His fullness. And He wants to do this for all His children! It starts with us letting Him remove untruth and letting Him completely have control. This does not happen in you all at once. Some days it is moment by moment and other times it is day by day. But as you let go and let God, your whole life changes for the good. This is what God means by going from glory to glory. You learn this or that about yourself or about God and then He takes you to the next level. Oh yeah, glory to glory!

> Yet grace (God's unmerited favor) was given to each of us individually [not indiscriminately, but in different ways] in proportion to the measure of Christ's [rich and bounteous] gift.
>
> —Ephesians 4:7

> His intention was the perfecting and the full equipping of the saints (His consecrated people), [that they should do] the work of ministering toward building

> up Christ's body (the church), [That it might develop] until we all attain oneness in the faith and in the comprehension of the [full and accurate] knowledge of the Son of God, that [we might arrive] at really mature manhood (the completeness of personality which is nothing less than the standard height of Christ's own perfection), the measure of the stature of the fullness of the Christ and the completeness found in Him.
>
> —EPHESIANS 4:12–13

Grace was given to us individually, in different ways but all in the proportion of His rich and bounteous gift. He is interested in perfecting us and equipping us for His work. We need to become one with Him and one with each other. He wants us mature in Him because "as He is, so are we in this world" (1 John 4:17). Jesus desires for all of us to have and operate as He did on Earth, in the fullness of God!

> Rather, let our lives lovingly express truth [in all things, speaking truly, dealing truly, living truly]. Enfolded in love, let us grow up in every way and in all things into Him Who is the Head, [even] Christ (the Messiah, the Anointed One).
>
> —EPHESIANS 4:15

Wow! God wants us to grow up this way in Him. Expressing truth in all things, in our speech, with how we deal with one another, and in how we live, all in love.

Chapter 6

ONE WITH CHRIST

Assuming that you have really heard Him and been taught by Him, as [all] Truth is in Jesus [embodied and personified in Him], strip yourselves of your former nature [put off and discard your old unrenewed self] which characterized your previous manner of life and becomes corrupt through lusts and desires that spring from delusion; And be constantly renewed in the spirit of your mind [having a fresh mental and spiritual attitude], and put on the new nature (the regenerate self) created in God's image, [Godlike] in true righteousness and holiness.

—*Ephesians 4:21–24*

THIS IS SOMETHING we really need to understand and do! We have to put down the flesh and pick up the new nature that God so graciously gives us. He wants us to be like Him—righteous and holy. Remember what Joyce Meyer taught about our new life? About the new you, how it comes right down from heaven into the old you, and how you need to tell the old you, "You are not rising again"?

> And become useful and helpful and kind to one another, tenderhearted (compassionate, understanding,

> loving-hearted), forgiving one another [readily and freely], as God in Christ forgave you.
>
> —Ephesians 4:32

This too is who we are in Christ!

> Therefore be imitators of God [copy Him and follow His example], as well-beloved children [imitate their father]. And walk in love, [esteeming and delighting in one another] as Christ loved us and gave Himself up for us, a slain offering and sacrifice to God [for you, so that it became] a sweet fragrance.
>
> —Ephesians 5:1–2

To be an imitator of God means to speak, act, and do just as He does. The only way this happens is to accept Jesus as Savior and Lord and live totally sold out to Him.

> For once you were darkness, but now you are light in the Lord; walk as children of Light [lead the lives of those native-born to the Light].
>
> —Ephesians 5:8

Do you recognize you are a child of the Light? This is part of renewing the mind. You speak of yourself as God speaks of you: "I am a child of the Light!"

> For the fruit (the effect, the product) of the Light or the Spirit [consists] in every form of kindly goodness, uprightness of heart, and trueness of life. And try to learn [in your experience] what is pleasing to the Lord [let your lives be constant proofs of what is most acceptable to Him].
>
> —Ephesians 5:9–10

Wow! The fruit, effect, and product of the Light is to do what pleases the Lord. In other words, think before you act or speak or do something.

> And do not get drunk with wine, for that is debauchery; but ever be filled and stimulated with the [Holy] Spirit.
>
> —Ephesians 5:18

> Do not associate with winebibbers; be not among them nor among gluttonous eaters of meat. [See also Isa. 5:22; Luke 21:34; Rom. 13:13.]
>
> —Proverbs 23:20

> In conclusion, be strong in the Lord, [be empowered through your union with Him]; draw your strength from Him [that strength which His boundless might provides].
>
> —Ephesians 6:10

In Him we are strong—empowered—and His strength is boundless! Read Ephesians 6:11–19 to see how we should operate in His power.

> And I am convinced and sure of this very thing, that He Who began a good work in you will continue until the day of Jesus Christ [right up to the time of His return], developing [that good work] and perfecting and bringing it to full completion in you....
>
> May you abound in and be filled with the fruits of righteousness (of right standing with God and right doing) which come through Jesus Christ (the Anointed One), to the honor and praise of God [that His glory may be both manifested and recognized].
>
> —Philippians 1:6, 11

This is God in us! He started this work in us and He will bring it to completion. He fills us with His righteousness to His honor and glory so that His glory will be manifested and recognized in us!

> This is in keeping with my own eager desire and persistent expectation and hope, that I shall not disgrace myself nor be put to shame in anything; but that with the utmost freedom of speech and unfailing courage, now as always heretofore, Christ (the Messiah) will be magnified and get glory and praise in this body of mine and be boldly exalted in my person, whether through (by) life or through (by) death. For me to live is Christ [His life in me], and to die is gain [the gain of the glory of eternity].
>
> —Philippians 1:20–21

My prayer is, "Lord be so in me/us that only You shine out of me/us!"

> So by whatever [appeal to you there is in our mutual dwelling in Christ, by whatever] strengthening and consoling and encouraging [our relationship] in Him [affords], by whatever persuasive incentive there is in love, by whatever participation in the [Holy] Spirit [we share], and by whatever depth of affection and compassionate sympathy, fill up and complete my joy by living in harmony and being of the same mind and one in purpose, having the same love, being in full accord and of one harmonious mind and intention....
>
> Let this same attitude and purpose and [humble] mind be in you which was in Christ Jesus [Let Him be your example in humility].
>
> —Philippians 2:1–2, 5

This same joy, compassion, sympathy, and affection will fill us up and give us one mind. Lord, that they may be one as

We are One (John 17:21). Same attitude (mind) of Jesus in me! Just like Him!

> [Not in your own strength] for it is God Who is all the while effectually at work in you [energizing and creating in you the power and desire], both to will and to work for His good pleasure and satisfaction and delight.
>
> —PHILIPPIANS 2:13

This is what God in you and me will do through us. Things will not get done in our strength but in His. "Both to will and to work for His good pleasure and satisfaction and delight."

> But whatever former things I had that might have been gains to me, I have come to consider as [one combined] loss for Christ's sake. Yes, furthermore, I count everything as loss compared to the possession of the priceless privilege (the overwhelming preciousness, the surpassing worth, and supreme advantage) of knowing Christ Jesus my Lord and of progressively becoming more deeply and intimately acquainted with Him [of perceiving and recognizing and understanding Him more fully and clearly]. For His sake I have lost everything and consider it all to be mere rubbish (refuse, dregs), in order that I may win (gain) Christ (the Anointed One), and that I may [actually] be found and known as in Him, not having any [self-achieved] righteousness that can be called my own, based on my obedience to the Law's demands (ritualistic uprightness and supposed right standing with God thus acquired), but possessing that [genuine righteousness] which comes through faith in Christ (the Anointed One), the [truly] right standing with God, which comes from God by [saving] faith. [For my determined purpose is] that I may know Him [that I may progressively

> become more deeply and intimately acquainted with Him, perceiving and recognizing and understanding the wonders of His Person more strongly and more clearly], and that I may in that same way come to know the power outflowing from His resurrection [which it exerts over believers], and that I may so share His sufferings as to be continually transformed [in spirit into His likeness even] to His death, [in the hope] that if possible I may attain to the [spiritual and moral] resurrection [that lifts me] out from among the dead [even while in the body]. Not that I have now attained [this ideal], or have already been made perfect, but I press on to lay hold of (grasp) and make my own, that for which Christ Jesus (the Messiah) has laid hold of me and made me His own.
>
> I do not consider, brethren, that I have captured and made it my own [yet]; but one thing I do [it is my one aspiration]: forgetting what lies behind and straining forward to what lies ahead, I press on toward the goal to win the [supreme and heavenly] prize to which God in Christ Jesus is calling us upward. So let those [of us] who are spiritually mature and full-grown have this mind and hold these convictions; and if in any respect you have a different attitude of mind, God will make that clear to you also.
>
> —Philippians 3:7–15

Wow! It is quite enlightening to pray this word over yourself. And the more you pray it the stronger it becomes in you!

> And God's peace [shall be yours, that tranquil state of a soul assured of its salvation through Christ, and so fearing nothing from God and being content with its earthly lot of whatever sort that is, that peace] which transcends all understanding shall garrison and mount guard over your hearts and minds in Christ Jesus.
>
> —Philippians 4:7

> I have strength for all things in Christ Who empowers me [I am ready for anything and equal to anything through Him Who infuses inner strength into me; I am self-sufficient in Christ's sufficiency].
>
> —PHILIPPIANS 4:13

> And my God will liberally supply (fill to the full) your every need according to His riches in glory in Christ Jesus.
>
> —PHILIPPIANS 4:19

Let's see; God has placed His peace in us, the peace that protects our minds and our hearts. He has strengthened us for whatever task He requires us to do for Him. Not only that, but He liberally supplies our every need to accomplish that task. This is the God who lives in us! Are you getting this?

> For this reason we also, from the day we heard of it, have not ceased to pray and make [special] request for you, [asking] that you may be filled with the full (deep and clear) knowledge of His will in all spiritual wisdom [in comprehensive insight into the ways and purposes of God] and in understanding and discernment of spiritual things—that you may walk (live and conduct yourselves) in a manner worthy of the Lord, fully pleasing to Him and desiring to please Him in all things, bearing fruit in every good work and steadily growing and increasing in and by the knowledge of God [with fuller, deeper, and clearer insight, acquaintance, and recognition]. [We pray] that you may be invigorated and strengthened with all power according to the might of His glory, [to exercise] every kind of endurance and patience (perseverance and forbearance) with joy, giving thanks to the Father, Who has qualified and made us fit to share the portion which is the inheritance of the saints (God's

> holy people) in the Light. [The Father] has delivered and drawn us to Himself out of the control and the dominion of darkness and has transferred us into the kingdom of the Son of His love, in Whom we have our redemption *through His blood,* [which means] the forgiveness of our sins.
>
> —Colossians 1:9–14, emphasis added

This too is a powerful prayer to pray over yourself. He has delivered us out of the control and dominion of darkness and transferred us into the kingdom of His Son. Recognize and believe what He says. I pray this prayer quite often. The Word works and this is how Jesus wants to be in us!

> Yet now has [Christ, the Messiah] reconciled [you to God] in the body of His flesh through death, in order to present you holy and faultless and irreproachable in His [the Father's] presence.
>
> —Colossians 1:22

Reconciled by Christ in order to present us holy and faultless and irreproachable before God!

> The mystery of which was hidden for ages and generations [from angels and men], but is now revealed to His holy people (the saints), to whom God was pleased to make known how great for the Gentiles are the riches of the glory of this mystery, which is Christ within and among you, the Hope [of realizing the] glory. Him we preach and proclaim, warning and admonishing everyone and instructing everyone in all wisdom (comprehensive insight into the ways and purposes of God), that we may present every person mature (full-grown, fully initiated, complete, and perfect) in Christ (the Anointed One).
>
> —Colossians 1:26–28

The mystery hidden but now revealed is Christ in us! We preach and proclaim only Him and we desire that all will become mature in Him. Not only do we desire this, but God the Father and Jesus and the Holy Spirit desire it too—even more than we do! God wants His children fully mature.

> [For my concern is] that their hearts may be braced (comforted, cheered, and encouraged) as they are knit together in love, that they may come to have all the abounding wealth and blessings of assured conviction of understanding, and that they may become progressively more intimately acquainted with and may know more definitely and accurately and thoroughly that mystic secret of God, [which is] Christ (the Anointed One). In Him all the treasures of [divine] wisdom (comprehensive insight into the ways and purposes of God) and [all the riches of spiritual] knowledge and enlightenment are stored up and lie hidden.
>
> —Colossians 2:2–3

We need to know Him more intimately. These words are for us to pray so we become more like Him. The only one who does not understand what God is saying about us in these verses is the one who does not know Him. God desires us to have knowledge of Him and insight into His will. We need to be in Him and then we will receive all He has.

> As you have therefore received Christ, [even] Jesus the Lord, [so] walk (regulate your lives and conduct yourselves) in union with and conformity to Him. Have the roots [of your being] firmly and deeply planted [in Him, fixed and founded in Him], being continually built up in Him, becoming increasingly more confirmed and established in the faith, just as you were taught, and abounding and overflowing in it with thanksgiving.
>
> —Colossians 2:6–7

If you've accepted Jesus as Savior you have received Him. So walk and conduct yourself in union and conformity to Him. Pray these words over yourself. Put yourself into the equation. Say, "I have received Christ; I am in union with Him; I am rooted and firmly planted in Him; I am being built up in Him; I am becoming increasingly more confirmed and established in my faith; I am abounding and overflowing in it with thanksgiving."

> For in Him the whole fullness of Deity (the Godhead) continues to dwell in bodily form [giving complete expression of the divine nature]. And you are in Him, made full and having come to fullness of life [in Christ you too are filled with the Godhead—Father, Son and Holy Spirit—and reach full spiritual stature]. And He is the Head of all rule and authority [of every angelic principality and power]. In Him you were circumcised with a circumcision not made with hands, but in a [spiritual] circumcision [performed by] Christ by stripping off the body of the flesh (the whole corrupt, carnal nature with its passions and lusts)....And you who were dead in trespasses and in the uncircumcision of your flesh (your sensuality, your sinful carnal nature), [God] brought to life together with [Christ], having [freely] forgiven us all our transgressions.
>
> —Colossians 2:9–11, 13

All the fullness of God is in us! Wow! Have you ever thought you were circumcised by Christ? This means the stripping off the body your whole corrupt, carnal nature—this is what we are in Him! Renewed! His nature lives in us! We were dead in our flesh (carnal nature) and God brought us back to life in Christ and forgave us all our transgressions. This is the rebirth!

Chapter 7

A NEW CREATION

If then you have been raised with Christ [to a new life, thus sharing His resurrection from the dead], aim at and seek the [rich, eternal treasures] that are above, where Christ is, seated at the right hand of God. And set your minds and keep them set on what is above (the higher things), not on the things that are on the earth. For [as far as this world is concerned] you have died, and your [new, real] life is hidden with Christ in God.

—*Colossians 3:1–3*

Have you been raised with Christ? Do you understand that your old self went to the grave (died) with Jesus? And when He arose to His new life, He gave that new life to us who accept Him.

> And have clothed yourselves with the new [spiritual self], which is [ever in the process of being] renewed and remolded into [fuller and more perfect knowledge upon] knowledge after the image (the likeness) of Him Who created it.
>
> —Colossians 3:10

Do you recognize you are a new spiritual being? Do you realize that you are continually being renewed and remolded into His image?

> Clothe yourselves therefore, as God's own chosen ones (His own picked representative), [who are] purified and holy and well-beloved [by God Himself, by putting on behavior marked by] tenderhearted pity and mercy, kind feeling, a lowly opinion of yourselves, gentle ways, [and] patience [which is tireless and long-suffering, and has the power to endure whatever comes, with good temper]. Be gentle and forbearing with one another and, if one has a difference (a grievance or complaint) against another, readily pardoning each other; even as the Lord has [freely] forgiven you, so must you also [forgive]. And above all these [put on] love and enfold yourselves with the bond of perfectness [which binds everything together completely in ideal harmony]. And let the peace (soul harmony which comes) from Christ rule (act and umpire continually) in your hearts [deciding and settling with finality all questions that arise in your minds, in that peaceful state] to which as [members of Christ's] one body you were also called [to live]. And be thankful (appreciative), [giving praise to God always]. Let the word [spoken by] Christ (the Messiah) have its home [in your hearts and minds] and dwell in you in [all its] richness, as you teach and admonish and train one another in all insight and intelligence and wisdom [in spiritual things, and as you sing] psalms and hymns and spiritual songs, making melody to God with [His] grace in your hearts. And whatever you do [no matter what it is] in word or deed, do everything in the name of the Lord Jesus and in [dependence upon] His Person, giving praise to God the Father through Him.
>
> —Colossians 3:12–17

This is an important word to pray over yourself. Put yourself into it and watch and see how you will grow in Him! Pray these words and He will see to it that it becomes you. You are saying what He is saying about you when you pray these words!

> Epaphras, who is one of yourselves, a servant of Christ Jesus, sends you greetings. [He is] always striving for you earnestly in his prayers, [pleading] that you may [as persons of ripe character and clear conviction] stand firm and mature [in spiritual growth], convinced and fully assured in everything willed by God.
>
> —Colossians 4:12

Wow! What a word to pray over yourself!

> But just as we have been approved by God to be entrusted with the glad tidings (the Gospel), so we speak not to please men but to please God, Who tests our hearts [expecting them to be approved].
>
> —1 Thessalonians 2:4

> And we also [especially] thank God continually for this, that when you received the message of God [which you heard] from us, you welcomed it not as the word of [mere] men, but as it truly is, the Word of God, which is effectually at work in you who believe [exercising its superhuman power in those who adhere to and trust in and rely on it].
>
> —1 Thessalonians 2:13

We speak of God to please God so others will learn about Him and accept Him. He tests us and approves us. He is at work in us and He gives us superhuman power to do what He desires done.

> And may the Lord make you increase and excel and overflow in love for one another and for all people, just as we also do for you, so that He may strengthen and confirm and establish your hearts faultlessly pure and unblamable in holiness in the sight of our God and Father, at the coming of our Lord Jesus Christ (the Messiah) with all His saints (the holy and glorified people of God)! Amen, (so be it)!
>
> —1 Thessalonians 3:12–13

God wants us to increase and excel and overflow in love for all. He desires to strengthen and confirm and establish us faultless and pure and unblamable, holy in His sight. right up to the time of Jesus' coming. He says we are a holy and glorified people. Do you realize this?

> And may the God of peace Himself sanctify you through and through [separate you from profane things, make you pure and wholly consecrated to God]; and may your spirit and soul and body be preserved sound and complete [and found] blameless at the coming of our Lord Jesus Christ (the Messiah). Faithful is He Who is calling you [to Himself] and utterly trustworthy, and He will also do it [fulfill His call by hallowing and keeping you].
>
> —1 Thessalonians 5:23–24

One should pray this word over oneself as well; and believe it is so because God said it! Put the "me" into it! "And may the God of peace Himself sanctify *me* through and through….and He will fulfill His call….and keep *me*."

> When He comes to be glorified in His saints [on that day He will be made more glorious in His consecrated people], and [He will] be marveled at and admired [in His glory reflected] in all who have believed [who have adhered to, trusted in, and relied on Him],

> because our witnessing among you was confidently accepted and believed [and confirmed in your lives]. With this in view we constantly pray for you, that our God may deem and count you worthy of [your] calling and [His] every gracious purpose of goodness, and with power may complete in [your] every particular work of faith (faith which is that leaning of the whole human personality on God in absolute trust and confidence in His power, wisdom, and goodness). Thus may the name of our Lord Jesus Christ be glorified and become more glorious through and in you, and may you [also be glorified] in Him according to the grace (favor and blessing) of our God and the Lord Jesus Christ (the Messiah, the Anointed One).
>
> —2 Thessalonians 1:10–12

We are His saints, His consecrated people. We reflect Him. We lean totally on Him in trust and confidence asking and praying that Jesus be glorified. He gives us grace (favor and spiritual blessing) because when we look good it makes Him look good!

> But we, brethren beloved by the Lord, ought and are obligated [as those who are in debt] to give thanks always to God for you, because God chose you from the beginning *as His firstfruits* (*first converts*) for salvation through the sanctifying work of the [Holy] Spirit and [your] belief in (adherence to, trust in, and reliance on) the Truth. [It was] to this end that He called you through our Gospel, so that you may obtain and share in the glory of our Lord Jesus Christ (the Messiah). So then, brethren, stand firm and hold fast to the traditions and instructions which you were taught by us, whether by our word of mouth or by letter. Now may our Lord Jesus Christ Himself and God our Father, Who loved us and gave us everlasting

> consolation and encouragement and well-founded hope through [His] grace (unmerited favor), comfort and encourage your hearts and strengthen them [make them steadfast and keep them unswerving] in every good work and word.
>
> —2 Thessalonians 2:13–17

Good words of encouragement to pray over yourself!

> Yet the Lord is faithful and He will strengthen [you] and set you on a firm foundation and guard you from the evil [one]....May the Lord direct your hearts into [realizing and showing] the love of God and into the steadfastness and patience of Christ and in waiting for His return.
>
> —2 Thessalonians 3:3, 5

These are also excellent words to pray over yourself!

> Now may the Lord of peace Himself grant you His peace (the peace of His kingdom) at all times and in all ways [under all circumstances and conditions, whatever comes]. The Lord [be] with you all....The grace (spiritual blessing and favor) of our Lord Jesus Christ (the Messiah) be with you all. Amen (so be it).
>
> —2 Thessalonians 3:16, 18

By now you should really understand this is Christ in you, and who you really are!

> Nor to give importance to or occupy themselves with legends (fables, myths) and endless genealogies, which foster and promote useless speculations and questionings rather than acceptance in faith of God's administration and the divine training that is in faith (in that leaning of the entire human personality on God in absolute trust and confidence).
>
> —1 Timothy 1:4

God accepts us by our faith in Him; we just need to realize this. Not only does He accept us but also He divinely administers direction and training in this faith (the "entire human personality on God in absolute trust and confidence"). He does not leave us alone. We need to get to that point where no matter what, God is first and we know He is the answer. Pray that you really know God has accepted you.

> I give thanks to Him Who has granted me [the needed] strength and made me able [for this], Christ Jesus our Lord, because He has judged and counted me faithful and trustworthy, appointing me [this stewardship of] the ministry.
>
> —1 Timothy 1:12

Do you realize He has granted to you the strength and made you able through Jesus to do what He has designed for you to do? One needs to say over oneself, "I am in the strength of Jesus my Lord; I have been judged and counted faithful and trustworthy to be a steward of the ministry He has given me." Saying His Word over yourself is powerful and God likes to hear it. He says, "My Word will not return unto Me void" (Isa. 55:11).

> Though I formerly blasphemed and persecuted and was shamefully and outrageously and aggressively insulting [to Him], nevertheless, I obtained mercy because I had acted out of ignorance in unbelief. And the grace (unmerited favor and blessing) of our Lord [actually] flowed out superabundantly and beyond measure for me, accompanied by faith and love that are [to be realized] in Christ Jesus. The saying is sure and true and worthy of full and universal acceptance, that Christ Jesus (the Messiah) came into the world to save sinners, of whom I am foremost. But I obtained mercy for the reason that in me, as the foremost [of

> sinners], Jesus Christ might show forth and display all His perfect long-suffering and patience for an example to [encourage] those who would thereafter believe on Him for [the gaining of] eternal life.
>
> —1 TIMOTHY 1:13–16

Mercy came to us even though we did not deserve it. But praise be to Jesus who shed His blood so we can live in His favor and blessing by faith and love in Him. It is only through Him. So realize you have obtained mercy through believing and accepting Jesus! This is to show to others He is waiting patiently for them to accept Him and to encourage them. If God can save and a change a sinner like me, He can most certainly do the same for you. Recognize you are no longer your old sinful self; you are a new creation as the Word says!

> For those who perform well as deacons acquire a good standing for themselves and also gain much confidence and freedom and boldness in the faith which is [founded on and centered] in Christ Jesus.
>
> —1 TIMOTHY 3:13

To be a deacon is to be totally sold out to God. God is so in you that only He comes out of you. His way of being and doing right is in you and you act and do as God acts and does. When you are at this point in letting Him be totally in you then you speak and act in that faith with confidence, freedom, and boldness because you have become totally "founded and centered" on Jesus! We all have the ability to operate in this kind of faith! Hebrews 4:16 tells us, "Let us then fearlessly and confidently and boldly draw near to the throne of grace (the throne of God's unmerited favor to us sinners,) that we may receive mercy [for our failures] and find grace to help in good time for every need [appropriate help and well-timed help, coming just when we need it]." Also Hebrews 13:6, "So we take comfort and are encouraged and confidently and boldly say,

The Lord is my Helper; I will not be seized with alarm [I will not fear or dread or be terrified]. What can man do to me?" This is our right in Him!

> So you, my son, be strong (strengthened inwardly) in the grace (spiritual blessing) that is [to be found only] in Christ Jesus.
>
> —2 TIMOTHY 2:1

Pray this word over yourself! Every time I have written "pray this word over yourself," it is because I have learned to put myself into the Word so my mind can be renewed to think, speak, and believe as God thinks, speaks, and believes.

> But the firm foundation of (laid by) God stands, sure and unshaken, bearing this seal (inscription): The Lord knows those who are His, and, Let everyone who names [himself by] the name of the Lord give up all iniquity and stand aloof from it.
>
> —2 TIMOTHY 2:19

This is an excellent scripture to remind yourself. You can pray it like this: "I am built on the firm foundation laid by God and it stands sure and unshaken. The Lord knows me and I bear His seal. I call myself by the name of the Lord and I choose to not commit iniquity and I move away from it. Amen—so be it."

> And how from your childhood you have had a knowledge of and been acquainted with the sacred Writings, which are able to instruct you and give you the understanding for salvation which comes through faith in Christ Jesus [through the leaning of the entire human personality on God in Christ Jesus in absolute trust and confidence in His power, wisdom, and goodness]. Every Scripture is God-breathed (given by His inspiration) and profitable for instruction, for reproof and

> conviction of sin, for correction of error and discipline in obedience, [and] for training in righteousness (in holy living, in conformity to God's will in thought, purpose, and action).
>
> —2 Timothy 3:15–16

Why does God do this? So we can live productive lives honoring Him in all He has for us to do! He teaches us and prepares us for our assignment, that assignment He pre-ordained before time began. If we are willing to listen and obey Him, we will learn how He wants us to operate and when the time comes to go out and do what He wants done, we will be thoroughly prepared.

> Paul, a bond servant of God and an apostle (a special messenger) of Jesus Christ (the Messiah) to stimulate and promote the faith of God's chosen ones and to lead them on to accurate discernment and recognition of and acquaintance with the Truth which belongs to and harmonizes with and tends to godliness.
>
> —Titus 1:1

His Word in us will stimulate and promote the faith of God in us and do as the rest of the sentence says. We will have accurate discernment and recognition of the Truth, and be God-like!

> And [now] in His own appointed time He has made manifest (made known) His Word and revealed it as His message through the preaching entrusted to me by command of God our Savior.
>
> —Titus 1:3

He has made known His Word and revealed His message by command of God our Savior. God does not just reveal His Word to a chosen few, but He reveals it to all who will hear! That means you and me, if we are listening.

> But when the goodness and loving-kindness of God our Savior to man [as man] appeared, He saved us, not because of any works of righteousness that we had done, but because of His own pity and mercy, by [the] cleansing [bath] of the new birth (regeneration) and renewing of the Holy Spirit, which He poured out [so] richly upon us through Jesus Christ our Savior. [And He did it in order] that we might be justified by His grace (by His favor, wholly undeserved), [that we might be acknowledged and counted as conformed to the divine will in purpose, thought, and action], and that we might become heirs of eternal life according to [our] hope.
>
> —TITUS 3:4–7

Just how did we get to be "in Christ"? Only by God through His Son. We didn't do a thing to deserve redemption; Jesus did it all! But as we accept Jesus as our Savior He cleanses us, and the Holy Spirit, which Jesus told us was coming, makes us new. (Remember the 120 waiting in the upper room. We too have access to that kind of infilling of the Holy Spirit.) He justified us by His grace so we might be conformed to His will in purpose, thought, and action. All to the hope of eternal life with Him. So do you really know you are saved, cleansed, reborn, infilled with the Holy Spirit, justified, and conformed to His divine will? This is what He says you are! And if He is saying this about you, why aren't you?

> [And I pray] that the participation in and sharing of your faith may produce and promote full recognition and appreciation and understanding and precise knowledge of every good [thing] that is ours in [our identification with] Christ Jesus [and unto His glory].
>
> —PHILEMON 6

Wow! Faith that produces and promotes to full recognition; as well as full appreciation and understanding, precise knowledge of who we are in Christ Jesus (our true identity). Oh, how wonderful God is to tell us who we are in Him! Recognize your new self and proclaim it in Jesus' name!

> [Besides this evidence] it was also established and plainly endorsed by God, Who showed His approval of it by signs and wonders and various miraculous manifestations of [His] power and by imparting the gifts of the Holy Spirit [to the believers] according to His own will.
>
> —Hebrews 2:4

God's plan for us. Miraculous manifestations of His power and impartation of the gifts of the Holy Spirit to all believers according to His will. This is Jesus in you, working through you!

> But Christ (the Messiah) was faithful over His [own Father's] house as a Son [and Master of it]. And it is we who are [now members] of this house, if we hold fast and firm to the end our joyful and exultant confidence and sense of triumph in our hope [in Christ].
>
> —Hebrews 3:6

Wow! We are members of His house! Hold fast and firm to Him.

> For we have become fellows with Christ (the Messiah) and share in all He has for us, if only we hold our first newborn confidence and original assured expectation [in virtue of which we are believers] firm and unshaken to the end.
>
> —Hebrews 3:14

Do you think of yourself as a fellow heir with Christ? We are when He becomes our Savior and Lord. Hold fast to Him and don't be shaken! This is something to think about. *The Dake Annotated Reference Bible* has a footnote concerning this verse. I think it worth writing out:

> After warning Christians that they can fall into sin and apostasy and be cut off from God by sin, as Israel was, the apostle lays down the condition they must meet to be finally saved. It is to hold the original confidence steadfast unto the end (v14).[1]

Which takes us to another footnote and a section called "Liberty in Prayer," in which Dake writes:

> Gr. parrhesia, freedom of speech; liberty of access to God. See note o, Acts 4:13. Here it refers to absolute confidence of access to God because all sins which separated from God are removed (Isa. 59:1-2). In O.T. days men were not permitted to approach God. Even the mountain on which God gave the law was not to be touched by man or beast. Only the high priest was permitted in the holy of holies once a year; and even then he could not approach God without proper atonement. Now, we all have free and daily access to God by the blood of Jesus (Heb. 10:19-23; Eph. 2:18). We are invited to come boldly to the throne of grace to obtain help in time of need (Heb. 4:14-16). As long as we hold fast to this liberty of access to God we are His house (v6). If sin is in the life we do not and cannot have this liberty of access. God will not hear our prayers (1 Jn. 3:20-22; 5:14–15). See Ps. 66:18.[2]

So we walk in liberty, having access to God every moment of the day. Don't stop talking to Him!

> For indeed we have had the glad tidings [Gospel of God] proclaimed to us just as truly as they [the Israelites of old did when the good news of deliverance from bondage came to them]; but the message they heard did not benefit them, because it was not mixed with faith (with the leaning of the entire personality on God in absolute trust and confidence in His power, wisdom, and goodness) by those who heard it; *neither were they united in faith with the ones [Joshua and Caleb] who heard (did believe)*. For we who have believed (adhered to and trusted in and relied on God) do enter that rest, in accordance with His declaration that those [who did not believe] should not enter when He said, As I swore in my wrath, They shall not enter My rest; and this He said although [His] works had been completed and prepared [and waiting for all who would believe] from the foundation of the world.
>
> —Hebrews 4:2–3

When we are in Christ, we are in His rest!

> But we do [strongly and earnestly] desire for each of you to show the same diligence and sincerity [all the way through] in realizing and enjoying the full assurance and development of [your] hope until the end, in order that you may not grow disinterested and become [spiritual] sluggards, but imitators, behaving as do those who through faith (by their leaning of the entire personality on God in Christ in absolute trust and confidence in His power, wisdom, and goodness) and by practice of patient endurance and waiting are [now] inheriting the promises.
>
> —Hebrews 6:11–12

We need to be diligent in our faith in Jesus, developing our hope totally in Him. How do we do this? Read, study, and believe the Word! In Christ I imitate Him and am *now* inheriting the promises. All the promises!

> I will imprint My laws upon their minds, even upon their innermost thoughts and understanding, and engrave them upon their hearts; and I will be their God, and they shall be My people. And it will nevermore be necessary for each one to teach his neighbor and his fellow citizen or each one his brother, saying, Know (perceive, have knowledge of, and get acquainted by experience with) the Lord, for all will know Me, from the smallest to the greatest of them. For I will be merciful and gracious toward their sins and I will remember their deeds of unrighteousness no more. When God speaks of a new [covenant or agreement], He makes the first one obsolete (out of use). And what is obsolete (out of use and annulled because of age) is ripe for disappearance and to be dispensed with altogether.
>
> —Hebrews 8:10b–13

God's laws are written on our hearts, even before we may become acquainted with Him. They are there! But oh what joy when we recognize they are and that He wants to live in us. So the Old Testament way of doing things is obsolete and the new has come through Jesus dying once for all sin and all sinners. Remember He is past, present, and future; so when we accept Him as our Savior, what sins are forgiven? *All our sins*, past, present, and future. As I have stated before, we ask for forgiveness when we have messed up after accepting Jesus not because God hasn't forgiven us, but because we don't want to do things that are not glorifying to Him. So if you are thinking you are an absolute mess up and ugly sinner because of a sin you committed today, let me reassure you that is not what God thinks of you! His thoughts toward you are good thoughts. No, He doesn't like the fact that you just messed up, but He does want you to learn from this mistake so you won't do it again. Neither does He look down from heaven at what you just did and say, "Well there goes forgiveness for him!" No! God is so loving toward His children and will always teach us how to live in Him. So just say, "Lord, forgive me, I don't want to do this." God is like an earthly father who will take his son aside and lovingly tell him, "This is not correct behavior; let's do something about this." God is in you and He wants everything just perfect for you!

Chapter 8

PURIFIED BY THE BLOOD

He went once for all into the [Holy of] Holies [of heaven], not by virtue of the blood of goats and calves [by which to make reconciliation between God and man], but His own blood, having found and secured a complete redemption (an everlasting release for us).

—*Hebrews 9:12*

Jesus did this for all. With His blood He found, secured, and completely redeemed us all! I think of the song we sing, "I've been redeemed by the blood of the Lamb." This is who we are in Him—redeemed!

> How much more surely shall the blood of Christ, Who by virtue of [His] eternal Spirit [His own preexistent divine personality] has offered Himself as an unblemished sacrifice to God, purify our consciences from dead works and lifeless observances to serve the [ever] living God? [Christ, the Messiah] is therefore the Negotiator and Mediator of an [entirely] new agreement (testament, covenant), so that those who are called and offered it may receive the fulfillment of the promised everlasting inheritance—since a death has taken place which rescues and delivers

> and redeems them from the transgressions committed under the [old] first agreement.
>
> —Hebrews 9:14–15

Wow! Think of this: His blood purifies. We are called and offered this new life so that we receive the fulfillment of all He has promised us. Not only that but He died and rose again so we can be rescued and delivered and redeemed. This is who we are in Him. We don't have to live like we are filthy, dirty sinners and will never be right until we see Him face-to-face. This is His promise for us right now! He is a right now God!

> Even so it is that Christ, having been offered to take upon Himself and bear as a burden the sins of man once and once for all, will appear a second time, not to carry any burden of sin nor to deal with sin, but to bring to full salvation those who are [eagerly, constantly, and patiently] waiting for and expecting Him.
>
> —Hebrews 9:28

Jesus was offered once for all men, once for all sins and sinners! Those of us who know Him as Savior are eagerly waiting for His return; but we are not stupid and do not have the mentality of, "I'm saved and as soon as He returns I'm out of here." We all should be doing what He has for us to do. What is it, you ask? The basic work of God is introducing others to Him.

> And in accordance with this will [of God], we have been made holy (consecrated and sanctified) through the offering made once for all of the body of Jesus Christ (the Anointed One).
>
> —Hebrews 10:10

Do you realize this is how God, Jesus, and the Holy Spirit look at you? You are holy! Consecrated! Sanctified! All by Jesus and what He did!

> This is the agreement (testament, covenant) that I will set up and conclude with them after those days, says the Lord: I will imprint My laws upon their hearts, and I will inscribe them on their minds (on their inmost thoughts, and understanding), He then goes on to say, And their sins and their lawbreaking I will remember no more. Now where there is absolute remission (forgiveness and cancellation of the penalty) of these [sins and lawbreaking], there is no longer any offering made to atone for sin. Therefore, brethren, since we have full freedom and confidence to enter into the [Holy of] Holies [by the power and virtue] in the blood of Jesus, by this fresh (new) and living way which He initiated and dedicated and opened for us through the separating curtain (veil of the Holy of Holies), that is, through His flesh, and since we have [such] a great and wonderful and noble Priest [Who rules] over the house of God, let us all come forward and draw near with true (honest and sincere) hearts in unqualified assurance and absolute conviction engendered by faith (by that leaning of the entire human personality on God in absolute trust and confidence in His power, wisdom, and goodness), having our hearts sprinkled and purified from a guilty (evil) conscience and our bodies cleansed with pure water. So let us seize and hold fast and retain without wavering the hope we cherish and confess and our acknowledgment of it, for He Who promised is reliable (sure) and faithful to His word.
>
> —Hebrews 10:16–23

Now look at who God says we are and what He says He does in us. He imprints His law on our hearts and minds. He no longer remembers the sins we did, or do (remember He died for all our sins, not just the ones of the past; the reason we ask for forgiveness after accepting Him is because we should not want to act in a way that does not glorify Him). In Him we have the freedom and should have the confidence to enter boldly into His throne room to ask of Him what we need or want, all because of Jesus' shed blood. He has given us the way to have honest and true hearts because He sprinkled and purified us with the blood of the Lamb, which is pure water. We have been cleansed. Hold fast to what God says about you, not what others say or you yourself say. Speak what God speaks!

> Do not be carried about by different and varied and alien teachings; for it is good for the heart to be established and ennobled and strengthened by means of grace (God's favor and spiritual blessing) and not [to be devoted to] foods [rules of diet and ritualistic meals], which bring no [spiritual] benefit or profit to those who observe them. We have an altar from which those who serve and worship in the tabernacle have no right to eat.
>
> —Hebrews 13:9–10

Now this is interesting. God wants our hearts to be established and ennobled and strengthened, but only by His grace! He does not want us to be distracted by rules and regulations of ritualistic ways of doing this or that.

Then Paul tells us God has a special altar at which those of the ritualistic kind have no right to eat:

> Through Him, therefore, let us constantly and at all times offer up to God a sacrifice of praise, which is the fruit of lips that thankfully acknowledge and confess and glorify His name.
>
> —Hebrews 13:15

Through Him we should constantly be praising God. Our lips at all times should only be speaking words of praise! I believe this is whether we are speaking about God Himself, or Jesus, or of the person who just cut in front of us on the road.

> Now may the God of peace [Who is the Author and the Giver of peace], Who brought again from among the dead our Lord Jesus, that great Shepherd of the sheep, by the blood [that sealed, ratified] the everlasting agreement (covenant, testament), strengthen (complete, perfect) and make you what you ought to be and equip you with everything good that you may carry out His will; [while He Himself] works in you and accomplishes that which is pleasing in His sight, through Jesus Christ (the Messiah); to Whom be the glory forever and ever (to the ages of the ages). Amen (so be it).
>
> —HEBREWS 13:20–21

I highly recommend you pray this over yourself! I really like the part that says He strengthens us, perfects us, and makes us what we ought to be, equipping us with everything good so we can carry out His will. This is Christ in us! And what works we do and accomplish in Him are pleasing to Father God!

> Blessed (happy, to be envied) is the man who is patient under trial and stands up under temptation, for when he has stood the test and been approved, he will receive [the victor's] crown of life which God has promised to those who love Him.
>
> —JAMES 1:12

> Every good gift and every perfect (free, large, full) gift is from above; it comes down from the Father of all [that gives] light, in [the shining of] Whom there can be no variation [rising or setting] or shadow cast by His turning [as in an eclipse].
>
> —JAMES 1:17

We are blessed even in the midst of a trial. When we come through we are approved, and when we get to heaven we receive a victor's crown! Not only that, but now we have access to every good gift in Him. Remember God is a right now God!

> And the harvest of righteousness (of conformity to God's will in thought and deed) is [the fruit of the seed] sown in peace by those who work for and make peace [in themselves and in others, that peace which means concord, agreement, and harmony between individuals, with undisturbedness, in a peaceful mind free from fears and agitating passions and moral conflicts].
>
> —James 3:18

The harvest of righteousness, which is conformity to God's will in all we do, is the fruit of His Seed, Jesus, which is sown in us. One of those seeds is righteousness, another is peace, a mind free from fears, agitating passions and conflict. Wow! That is Christ is us! We are righteous through Him! And the harvest is all God's attributes of love, joy, peace, long-suffering, patience, and so forth (Gal. 5:22–26).

> [You should] be exceedingly glad on this account, though now for a little while you may be distressed by trials and suffer temptations, so that [the genuineness] of your faith may be tested, [your faith] which is infinitely more precious than the perishable gold which is tested and purified by fire. [This proving of your faith is intended] to redound to [your] praise and glory and honor when Jesus Christ (the Messiah, the Anointed One) is revealed.
>
> —1 Peter 1:6–7

Our faith is tested, tried, and purified. How often we have to go into the fire is based on how quickly we learn what God is teaching. But when we are refined by fire we are totally renewed (that means all the junk is taken out), and this makes God look real good!

> And I will bring the third part through the fire, and will refine them as silver is refined and will test them as gold is tested. They will call on My name, and I will hear and answer them. I will say, It is My people; and they will say, The Lord is my God.
>
> —ZECHARIAH 13:9

> Behold, I have refined you, but not as silver; I have tried and chosen you in the furnace of affliction.
>
> —ISAIAH 48:10

So the next time you are going through something, stop and seek God, asking Him to reveal to you why this is going on. He does a thorough job when He refines. He wants to get the "junk" out!

> So brace up your minds; be sober (circumspect, morally alert); set your hope wholly and unchangeably on the grace (divine favor) that is coming to you when Jesus Christ (the Messiah) is revealed. [Live] as children of obedience [to God]; do not conform yourselves to the evil desires [that governed you] in your former ignorance [when you did not know the requirements of the Gospel]. But as the One Who called you is holy, you yourselves also be holy in all your conduct and manner of living. For it is written, You shall be holy, for I am holy.
>
> And if you call upon Him as [your] Father Who judges each one impartially according to what he does, [then] you should conduct yourselves with true reverence throughout the time of your temporary residence [on the earth, whether long or short]. You must know (recognize) that you were redeemed (ransomed) from the useless (fruitless) way of living

> inherited by tradition from [your] forefathers, not with corruptible things [such as] silver and gold, but [you were purchased] with the precious blood of Christ (the Messiah), like that of a [sacrificial] lamb without blemish or spot.
>
> —1 Peter 1:13–19

We are called to live as children obedient to God, holy as He is holy. We should be reverent to Him in all we do, for we are redeemed. We were purchased by His precious blood! Recognize this truth. It is His blood that did all this so we could be like Him!

> Through Him you believe in (adhere to, rely on) God, Who raised Him up from the dead and gave Him honor and glory, so that your faith and hope are [centered and rest] in God. Since by your obedience to the Truth *through the [Holy] Spirit* you have purified your hearts for the sincere affection of the brethren, [see that you] love one another fervently from a pure heart. You have been regenerated (born again), not from a mortal origin (seed, sperm), but from one that is immortal by the *ever* living and lasting Word of God.
>
> —1 Peter 1:21–23

This is who God says we are in Him. Our faith and hope are centered and rest in Him. We are obedient to the truth if we truly let the Holy Spirit purify us; we love one another with pure hearts. We have been regenerated by Jesus, who is "the ever living and lasting Word of God."

> [Come] and, like living stones, be yourselves built [into] a spiritual house, for a holy (dedicated, consecrated) priesthood, to offer up [those] spiritual sacrifices [that are] acceptable and pleasing to God through Jesus Christ. For thus it stands in Scripture:

> Behold, I am laying in Zion a chosen (honored), precious chief Cornerstone, and he who believes in Him [who adheres to, trusts in, and relies on Him] shall never be disappointed or put to shame. To you then who believe (who adhere to, trust in, and rely on Him) is the preciousness....
>
> But you are a chosen race, a royal priesthood, a dedicated nation, [God's] own purchased, special people, that you may set forth the wonderful deeds and display the virtues and perfections of Him Who called you out of darkness into His marvelous light. Once you were not a people [at all], but now you are God's people; once you were unpitied, but now you are pitied and have received mercy.
>
> —1 PETER 2:5–6, 7A, 9–10

A holy, dedicated, and consecrated people. When we believe in Him we shall never be disappointed or put to shame. We are a chosen race, a royal priesthood, and a dedicated nation, purchased by God—a special people—so we can show the wonderful deeds and display the virtues and perfections of Him. We are no longer in darkness but in His light! We are His people! We are pitied and have received mercy!

> He personally bore our sins in His [own] body on the tree [as on an altar and offered Himself on it], that we might die (cease to exist) to sin and live to righteousness. By His wounds you have been healed.
>
> —1 PETER 2:24

Do you see what He did for us? He personally bore our sins in His own body. He offered Himself so that we could die to sin and live to righteousness. Jesus was tempted in every way and did not sin (Heb. 4:15). Since He came to show us how we can live and He lives in us, then in Him we can choose to not sin, and therefore be just like Him. Through Him, only

Him, do we have the ability to do this. And some days it is a moment-by-moment learning. God will perfect this kind of living in us as we yield to Him (Phil. 1:6). Look closely at this verse and how it says, "we might die (cease to exist) to sin." That means it is our choice of truly letting Jesus live in us in every way and circumstance. Remember when you accepted Jesus as Savior, everything the Father gave Him to help Him succeed while He was in the flesh He gave to us so we can be just like Him in every way, including not sinning.

> But let it be the inward adorning and beauty of the hidden person of the heart, with the incorruptible and unfading charm of a gentle and peaceful spirit, which [is not anxious or wrought up, but] is very precious in the sight of God.
>
> —1 PETER 3:4

This is a good verse to pray over yourself, especially telling yourself you are "very precious in the sight of God."

Chapter 9

ONCE FOR ALL

For Christ [the Messiah Himself] died for sins once for all, the Righteous for the unrighteous (the Just for the unjust, the Innocent for the guilty), that He might bring us to God. In His human body He was put to death, but He was made alive in the spirit.

—*1 Peter 3:18*

Once for all. That includes all sins we have done and will do. God is past, present, and future. Time does not exist to Him. So once for all doesn't just mean for all mankind, which He did die for; it also means for all sins, whether committed in the past, today, or tomorrow.

> So, since Christ suffered in the flesh *for us, for you*, arm yourselves with the same thought and purpose [patiently to suffer rather than fail to please God]. For whoever has suffered in the flesh [having the mind of Christ] is done with [intentional] sin [has stopped pleasing himself and the world, and pleases God], so that he can no longer spend the rest of his natural life living by [his] human appetites and desires, but [he lives] for what God wills.
>
> —1 Peter 4:1–2, emphasis added

In Christ. Christ in us should mean we don't want to do anything unless it pleases God. It should mean that we don't want to "intentionally sin." Some people think like this: "I can do this sin because God loves me and has forgiven me," or, "Well I can ask for forgiveness later." What if there is no later for you? Choose to live sinless! And recognize this sinless life does not happen overnight; it takes practice. Once again I remind you we ask God to forgive us of sins we do after accepting Him as Savior, not because that sin will separate us from God forever, but because we recognize it is not pleasing to Him.

> But insofar as you are sharing Christ's sufferings, rejoice, so that when His glory [full of radiance and splendor] is revealed, you may also rejoice with triumph [exultantly].
>
> —1 Peter 4:13

Wow! Since we share His sufferings we also get to share His glory. Remember He says in John 17:22 that He has given us the glory that God gave Him. So get to know yourself and who you really are.

> Be well balanced (temperate, sober of mind), be vigilant and cautious at all times; for that enemy of yours, the devil, roams around like a lion roaring [in fierce hunger], seeking someone to seize upon and devour. Withstand him; be firm in faith [against his onset—rooted, established, strong, immovable, and determined], knowing that the same (identical) sufferings are appointed to your brotherhood (the whole body of Christians) throughout the world. And after you have suffered a little while, the God of all grace [Who imparts all blessing and favor], Who has called you to His [own] eternal glory in Christ Jesus, will Himself complete and make you what you

> ought to be, establish and ground you securely, and strengthen, and settle you.
>
> —1 Peter 5:8–10

All these things we can be in Him! And He will see to it that the work He has begun in us will be completed. We will be established; He will keep us in security; He will strengthen us and settle us. This is who we are in Him! Also look at Philippians 1:6.

> Salute one another with a kiss of love [the symbol of mutual affection]. To all of you that are in Christ Jesus (the Messiah), may there be peace (every kind of peace and blessing, especially peace with God, and freedom from fears, agitating passions, and moral conflicts. Amen (so be it).
>
> —1 Peter 5:14

These attributes of God are in us when we have accepted Him as Savior.

> May grace (God's favor) and peace (which is perfect well-being, all necessary good, all spiritual prosperity, and freedom from fears and agitating passions and moral conflicts) be multiplied to you in [the full, personal, precise, and correct] knowledge of God and of Jesus our Lord. For His divine power has bestowed upon us all things that [are requisite and suited] to life and godliness, through the [full, personal] knowledge of Him Who called us by and to His own glory and excellence (virtue). By means of these He has bestowed on us His precious and exceedingly great promises, so that through them you may escape [by flight] from the moral decay (rottenness and corruption) that is in the world because of covetousness (lust and greed), and become sharers (partakers) of the divine nature. For this very reason, adding your

> diligence [to the divine promises], employ every effort in exercising your faith to develop virtue (excellence, resolution, Christians energy), and in [exercising] virtue [develop] knowledge (intelligence), and in [exercising] knowledge [develop] self-control, and in [exercising] self-control [develop] steadfastness (patience, endurance), and in [exercising] steadfastness [develop] godliness (piety), and in [exercising] godliness [develop] brotherly affection, and in [exercising] brotherly affection [develop] Christian love. For these qualities are yours and increasingly abound in you, they will keep [you] from being idle or unfruitful unto the [full personal] knowledge of our Lord Jesus Christ (the Messiah, the Anointed One). For whoever lacks these qualities is blind, [spiritually] shortsighted, seeing only what is near to him, and has become oblivious [to the fact] that he was cleansed from his old sins. Because of this, brethren, be all the more solicitous and eager to make sure (to ratify, to strengthen, to make steadfast) your calling and election; for if you do this, you will never stumble or fall. Thus there will be richly and abundantly provided for you entry into the eternal kingdom of our Lord and Savior Jesus Christ.
>
> —2 Peter 1:2–11

These are powerful words that speak of whose we are, and who we are in Him!

> But grow in grace (undeserved favor, spiritual strength) and recognition and knowledge and understanding of our Lord and Savior Jesus Christ (the Messiah). To Him [be] glory (honor, majesty, and splendor) both now and to the day of eternity. Amen (so be it)!
>
> —2 Peter 3:18

Pray this word over yourself:

> If we [freely] admit that we have sinned and confess our sins, He is faithful and just (true to His own nature and promises) and will forgive our sins [dismiss our lawlessness] and [continuously] cleanse us from all unrighteousness [everything not in conformity to His will in purpose, thought, and action].
>
> —1 JOHN 1:9

This is how we get saved: admit we've sinned, confess our sins, and ask Him to come live in us. He does forgive our sins when we ask Him. Not only does He forgive us of our sins but He keeps continually cleansing us from all unrighteousness. "[Everything not in conformity to His will in purpose, thought, and action]." This is a really good deal! Don't pass it up! Cry out to Him if you have not done this.

> But you have been anointed by [you hold a sacred appointment from, you have been given an unction from] the Holy One, and you all know [the Truth] *or you know all things.*
>
> —1 JOHN 2:20

> But as for you, the anointing (the sacred appointment, the unction) which you received from Him abides [permanently] in you; [so] then you have no need that anyone should instruct you. But just as His anointing teaches you concerning everything and is true and is no falsehood, so you must abide in (live in, never depart from) Him [being rooted in Him, knit to Him], just as [His anointing] has taught you [to do]. And now, little children, abide (live, remain permanently) in Him, so that when He is made visible, we may have and enjoy perfect confidence (boldness, assurance) and not be ashamed and shrink from Him at His coming. If you know (perceive and are

> sure) that He [Christ] is [absolutely] righteous [conforming to the Father's will in purpose, thought, and action], you may also know (be sure) that everyone who does righteously [and is therefore in like manner conformed to the divine will] is born (begotten) of Him [God].
>
> —1 JOHN 2:27–29

We were anointed when we received Him as Savior and Lord. He came to live in us! He teaches us all things! We are rooted and knit in Him! We can come boldly before Him! And since we conform to His will we can assuredly know we are His.

> No one who abides in Him [who lives and remains in communion with and in obedience to Him—deliberately, knowingly, and habitually] commits (practices) sin. No one who [habitually] sins has either seen or known Him [recognized, perceived or understood Him, or has had an experiential acquaintance with Him].
>
> —1 JOHN 3:6

There is a difference between deliberate sin and just messing up. The difference is, when Jesus is in you and you mess up, a conviction of sorrow for what you have just done should come upon you. That is Jesus in you showing you He wants better for you. So ask Him to forgive you, and realize He does forgive. Don't drag yourself down with the words you say about yourself; build yourself up with what God says about you! Deliberate sin is just that: you do not care that you just did something that is unglorifying to God.

Chapter 10

ARE YOU LISTENING?

Little children, let us not love [merely] in theory or in speech but in deed and in truth (in practice and in sincerity). By this we shall come to know (perceive, recognize, and understand) that we are of the Truth, and can reassure (quiet, conciliate, and pacify) our hearts in His presence, whenever our hearts in [tormenting] self-accusation make us feel guilty and condemn us. [For we are in God's hands.] For He is above and greater than our consciences (our hearts), and He knows (perceives and understands) everything [nothing is hidden from Him]. And, beloved, if our consciences (our hearts) do not accuse us [if they do not make us feel guilty and condemn us], we have confidence (complete assurance and boldness) before God, and we receive from Him whatever we ask, because we [watchfully] obey His orders [observe His suggestions and injunctions, follow His plan for us] and [habitually] practice what is pleasing to Him.

—1 John 3:18–22

SO WHOM ARE you listening to? Are you listening to what God says about you? Or are you listening to what you say about yourself or what somebody else says about you? Quite often I have found that the devil dangles something in front of us, and if we don't recognize who we are in Jesus we will quickly take the bite and begin beating ourselves up and saying untruths of ourselves. Repent of this and speak what God says about you!

> Little children, you are of God [you belong to Him] and have [already] defeated and overcome them [the agents of the antichrist], because He Who lives in you is greater (mightier) than he who is in the world.
>
> —1 John 4:4

> We are [children] of God, Whoever is learning to know God [progressively to perceive, recognize, and understand God by observation and experience, and to get an ever-clearer knowledge of Him] listens to us; and he who is not of God does not listen or pay attention to us. By this we know (recognize) the Spirit of Truth and the spirit of error.
>
> —1 John 4:6

> In this the love of God was made manifest (displayed) where we are concerned: in that God sent His Son, the only begotten or unique [Son], into the world so that we might live through Him. In this is love: not that we loved God, but that He loved us and sent His Son to be the propitiation (the atoning sacrifice) for our sins.
>
> —1 John 4:9–10

> Anyone who confesses (acknowledges, owns) that Jesus is the Son of God, God abides (lives, makes His home) in him and he [abides, lives, makes his home] in God.
>
> —1 John 4:15

Do you see what God says about us in these verses? Because He lives in us and we live in Him we have already defeated the enemy. He lives in us! Because He lives in us we should be growing more intimately acquainted with Him, we should be growing in our knowledge of Him. If one is not growing in God, others who know God will recognize the Spirit of truth or the spirit of error about that one. Also, realize that one has to read and study and learn the Word to really know what God says. One can continue to be in error until they really begin to study the Word. God is an excellent teacher and if we are willing to learn He will teach us well, through the Word, as well as through teachers of the Word.

Recognize that God sent Jesus to be our sin offering because He loved us. He, as the above says, loved us and sent His Son to be the "atoning sacrifice for our sins." If we have confessed that Jesus is the Son of God and asked Him to forgive us of our sins, He forgave us of our sins and came to live in us. We also need to live in Him. Doing this is a moment-by-moment living some days. It is getting into the Word and learning who He is. These scriptures take us back to where I began studying who we are in Christ: John 17:23.

> And we know (understand, recognize, are conscious of, by observation and by experience) and believe (adhere to and put faith in and rely on the love God cherishes for us. God is love, and he who dwells and continues in love dwells and continues in God, and God dwells and continues in him. In this [union and communion with Him] love is brought to completion and attains perfection with us, that we may have confidence for the day of judgment [with assurance and boldness to face Him], because as He is, so are we in this world.
>
> —1 John 4:16–17

Do you really know God loves you? If not, stop and ask God to forgive you for not knowing His truth—that He loves you. Ask Him to fill you to full with Him, even if you have to keep repeating for the next three months, "God loves me." Because as you say these words, the word God says about you, you hear; and what you hear gets into you, and soon you will really know and believe He loves you (Rom. 10:17; Rev. 2:7)! Are you listening? Ask God to open your ears to hear what He has to say.

> Everyone who believes (adheres to, trusts, and relies on the fact) that Jesus is the Christ (the Messiah) is a born-again child of God; and everyone who loves the Father also loves the one born of Him (His offspring). By this we come to know (recognize and understand) that we love the children of God: when we love God and obey His commands (orders, charges)—[when we keep His ordinances and are mindful of His precepts and His teaching].
>
> —1 John 5:1–2

Do you love God? Do you love Jesus? If you do love them, you should recognize you are a child of God. Do you love others? Do you love yourself? Jesus was asked once, "What is the greatest commandment?" (Matt. 22:36). His reply was, "To love the Lord your God with all your heart, all your mind and all your soul. And the second is like it: to love your neighbor as you love yourself" (Matt. 22:37–39). If you do not love yourself it is hard to love anyone else. Talk to God about how you feel about yourself and begin to line up your thinking with His thinking. Say what He says you are in Him, not what you feel or what others have told you. Speak the Word until you are so "rooted and grounded" (Eph. 3:17) in it that it is the only Word that comes out of your mouth!

> For whatever is born of God is victorious over the world; and this is the victory that conquers the world, even our faith. Who is it that is victorious over [that conquers] the world but he who believes that Jesus is the Son of God [who adheres to, trusts in, and relies on that fact]?
>
> —1 John 5:4–5

> He who believes in the Son of God [who adheres to, trusts in, and relies on Him] has the testimony [possesses this divine attestation] within himself.
>
> —1 John 5:10a

> We know [absolutely] that anyone born of God does not [deliberately and knowingly] practice committing sin, but the One Who was begotten of God carefully watches over and protects him [Christ's divine presence within him preserves him against the evil], and the wicked one does not lay hold (get a grip) on him or touch [him].
>
> —1 John 5:18

So you are born again. Do you know you have been made victorious because Jesus lives in you? Since He lives in us we can choose to sin or not to sin. God in us gives us the victory to overcome any temptation that comes our way. God in us, us in God. All His divine attributes are in us, we just have to learn to grow in them and die daily to our flesh.

> Anyone who runs on ahead [of God] and does not abide in the doctrine of Christ [who is not content with what He taught] does not have God; but he who continues to live in the doctrine (teaching) of Christ [does have God], he has both the Father and the Son.
>
> —2 John 9

The doctrine that Christ taught is: "I came that they might have life" (John 10:10); "I gave Myself once for all mankind and for all sin" (Heb. 10:10); "I died and rose again and now sit at the right hand of God as High Priest pleading for you" (1 Cor. 5:4; 2 Cor. 5:15; Rom. 8:34; Eph. 1:20; Heb. 10:12; 12:2). The doctrine of Christ is that He came to earth as a baby, died on the cross as a sacrifice for all sin, was buried and rose on the third day, and now sits at the right hand of God, and the only way to get to live with Him is to have a personal relationship with Him as Savior and Lord (Rom. 10:13; 1 John 1:9). Any other gospel is not His gospel.

One needs to understand that this kind of believing on the Lord Jesus Christ as your Savior is not knowing about Him, it is much deeper than that; but not so deep you can't understand. God made the mind that is within all of us. He created every part of us—our bodies, our souls, and our spirits. He gave us our thinking power so we can comprehend all things and come to understand what is being taught. In Ephesians 3:18 Paul teaches, "That you may have the power and be strong to apprehend and grasp with all the saints [God's devoted people, the experience of that love] what is the breath and length and height and depth [of it]." It is God's will for us to understand and comprehend all His Son Jesus did for us. It is God's will for us to have complete knowledge of who He is and who we are in Him!

> Beloved, do not imitate evil, but imitate good. He who does good is of God; he who does evil has not seen (discerned or experienced) God [has enjoyed no vision of Him and does not know Him at all].
>
> —3 John 11

This goes back to doing only those things which please God, as well as being an imitator of God, as Ephesians 5:1 says, "Therefore be imitators of God [copy Him and follow

His example], as well-beloved children [imitate their father]." This is how we show He is in us and who we are in Him.

> Jude, a servant of Jesus Christ (the Messiah), and brother of James, [writes this letter] to those who are called (chosen), dearly loved by God the Father and separated (set apart) and kept for Jesus Christ.
>
> —JUDE 1

This too is a powerful word to speak over ourselves! We are servants of Jesus Christ; we are called and dearly loved by God and we are separated and kept for Jesus. This is a wonderful way to look at ourselves and tell the devil he is a liar. And he can no longer tell us we aren't good enough or loved. God our Father says we are!

Conclusion

WHO DO YOU SAY YOU ARE?

And they have overcome (conquered) him by means of the blood of the Lamb and by the utterance of their testimony, for they did not love and cling to life even when faced with death [holding their lives cheap till they had to die for their witnessing].

—REVELATION 12:11

WE ALL KNOW how powerful the blood of the Lamb is, or at least you should. Jesus' shed blood is so powerful that it heals, cleanses, delivers, strengthens, makes one bold, sets free, sanctifies, makes holy, preserves, protects, covers, and oh so much His blood does for us—you could fill pages upon pages. It is His blood that truly redeems and nothing else. So what about this utterance, or as the King James Bible says, "the word of their testimony"? What is the word of our testimony? Often churches have a testimony night and people tell what God has done for them—and believe me, what they share is a testimony! Our testimony can be how we found Jesus or some great thing He did for us, whether being healed or delivered. Or just a praise report of His greatness! And this is all good! However, I believe that the word of our testimony goes deeper than that. I believe the word of our testimony is foremost the words we speak about ourselves according to the Word. What a testimony to say I am redeemed, I am forgiven according to this verse found in whatever chapter and book of the Bible of which you speak. Remember God's Word does not return void unto Him (Isa. 55:11). So when we speak His words, as He speaks, there is power that goes with them and unfolds into our lives. Wow! What a testimony!

Let's look at two Scriptures. One found in Colossians 3:16, "Let every word [spoken by] Christ (the Messiah) have its home [in your hearts and minds] and dwell in you in [all its] richness, as you teach and admonish and train one another in all insight and intelligence and wisdom [in spiritual things, and as you sing] psalms and hymns and spiritual songs, making melody to God with [His] grace in your hearts." As well as 2 Corinthians 6:7, "By [speaking] the word of truth, in the power of God, with the weapons of righteousness for the right hand [to attack] and for the left hand [to defend]."

The Word of God is to have first place in our hearts and minds. We are to speak it! This is so we can learn it ourselves so we are able to teach it to others. Look at the power of the words spoken through our mouths; it is like a weapon for attacking and for defending. And the Word works! Remember what Moses taught about the Lord in Deuteronomy 28:7? "The Lord shall cause your enemies who rise up against you to be defeated before your face; they shall come out against you one way and flee before you seven ways." This is how the Word works in every situation. Once you understand who you are in Christ and begin speaking what He speaks, the enemy runs away! As 2 Corinthians 10:3–4 says, "For though we walk (live) in the flesh, we are not carrying on our warfare according to the flesh and using mere human weapons. For the weapons of our warfare are not physical [weapons of flesh and blood], but they are mighty before God for the overthrow and destruction of strongholds." Our weapons are one thing: the Word of God! The Word works!

There are many more scriptures found in the Old Testament that tell us who we are as well, such as Song of Solomon 2:16,

"[She said distinctly] My beloved is mine and I am His! He pastures his flocks among the lilies." Do you realize you are His beloved? Oh, yes, He loves you! Or Jeremiah 29:11, "For I know the thoughts and plans that I have for you, says the Lord, thoughts and plans for welfare and peace and not for evil, to give you hope in your final outcome." God loves us so much and His thoughts are for our good. If you are saying the opposite of what He says you are going to get what you say. So say, "God has good plans for me, for my welfare, and for my peace, and He gives me hope."

God knew you before you were even formed in your mother's womb (Ps. 139:15–16). David continues in verse 17 saying of the Lord, "How precious and weighty also are Your thoughts to me, O God! How vast is the sum of them!" Since God has good thoughts toward us for our good—and not just one thought but a vast sum—we need to read His Word to really see (and hear) what He says about us. We also need *to proclaim* what He says about us. Soon, as we begin saying out loud what God says we will see victory in what we are proclaiming about ourselves. As I have stated before, as we begin to say about ourselves what God says about us in His Word, He says, "So shall My word be that goes forth out of My mouth: it shall not return to Me void [without producing any effect, useless], but it shall accomplish that which I please and purpose, and it shall prosper in the thing for which I sent it" (Isa. 55:11), and His Word produces exactly what He says. So what are you saying?

We, the people of God, are His voice in this earth realm and He loves to hear us speak His Word over our lives. As we speak His Word it takes root and grows in us, accomplishing what His Word says about every situation we may be in.

My prayer is that you have come to really know who you are in Christ. If you have never accepted Jesus as your Savior pray this simple pray and ask Him into your life:

Jesus, I know I am a sinner and have sinned against You. Forgive me of all my sins. Come and dwell in me. Teach me about You. Live in me and be my Savior and Lord. Amen (so be it).

Repentance and forgiveness are that simple. Growing in Him takes time. But if you are willing to learn, He is so willing to teach. Talk the Word! And as Paul quite often ended his letters, I too end this with, "May the Lord Jesus be with you and bless you always. Amen (so be it)."

NOTES

Chapter 7: A New Creation

1. Finis Jennings Dake, *Dake's Annotated Reference Bible: The Old and New Testaments, with Notes, Concordance and Index* (Lawrenceville, GA: Dake Bible Sales, 1991), 246.

2. Ibid., 257.

ABOUT THE AUTHOR

Noreen and her husband, Jerry, have been married for thirty-four years, and have two children. They have lived in Williston, North Dakota, since 1987. God has taught Noreen through His Word, and especially who she really is in God's Son Jesus. Her desire is to bring God's revelation to others in her books.

CONTACT THE AUTHOR

P.O. Box 7586

Williston, North Dakota 58801